The Complete Guide to Log Homes

Clyde H. Cremer
Jeffrey S. Cremer

The Complete Guide to Log Homes:

How to Buy, Build, and Maintain Your Dream Home

Clyde H. Cremer
Jeffrey S. Cremer

iUniverse, Inc.
New York   Bloomington

The Complete Guide to Log Homes
How to Buy, Build, and Maintain Your Dream Home

Copyright © 2008 by Jeff Cremer

iUniverse books may be ordered through booksellers or by contacting:

iUniverse
1663 Liberty Drive
Bloomington, IN 47403
www.iuniverse.com
1-800-Authors (1-800-288-4677)

ISBN: 978-0-595-44143-3 (pbk)
ISBN: 978-0-595-68502-8 (cloth)
ISBN: 978-0-595-88467-4 (ebk)

Printed in the United States of America

Contents

Disclaimer

The authors have made every effort to produce a high-quality, informative book and to provide accurate information concerning the subject matter. However, the authors cannot guarantee that this book is free of errors, and it may contain typographical, content, and other inadvertent errors. The authors make no representations or warranties of any kind with regard to the accuracy, applicability, fitness, or completeness of the contents of this publication, and they expressly disclaim any and all liability for any errors or omissions.

This book is for informational purposes only. It should be used only as a general guide and not as the ultimate reference source. It is not a substitute for professional advice, which should always be sought in regard to the construction of an actual log home. Any recommendations in this publication are based on the authors' personal experiences and research and are believed to be reliable and accurate but not infallible. Any examples or illustrations presented in this publication have been chosen solely to demonstrate given points. The reader should conduct a thorough investigation of their applicability to the reader's individual circumstances.

The authors make no representations or warranties, whether express or implied, including, but not limited to, warranties of merchantability or fitness for a particular purpose, and all such representations and warranties are expressly disclaimed by the authors.

The authors assume no liability or responsibility to any person or entity with respect to any loss or damages (including but not limited to actual, compensatory, direct, indirect, incidental, punitive, or consequential damages) related or alleged to be related directly or indirectly to this publication or any use or application of the information contained in this publication.

Dedicated to

Brandon A. Melby

October 2, 1979 – May 12, 2004

During Brandon's ephemeral life, he bestowed a special craftsmanship on every home that he built. These homes will stand as a mute testimony to his skill, diligence, and devotion to his clients. His honesty and integrity are a tribute to his parents and grandparents, who transformed this youth into an adult of character.

Quiet like some still day. Going home, but not away.

Acknowledgments

We would like to thank the following people for their valuable contributions to the book:

Dr. David E. Kretschmann is the Research General Engineer in the Engineering Properties of Wood Research Work Unit at the U.S. Forest Products Laboratory in Madison, WI. David received his B.S. and M.S. in Engineering Mechanics from University of Wisconsin-Madison and is currently a Ph.D. candidate in the Civil and Environmental Engineering Department at the University of Wisconsin-Madison.

Dr. Robert H. White is a fire researcher at the US Forest Service Forest Products Laboratory, Madison, WI.

Mr. Norman Kolpas is an honors graduate of Yale University. As author, writer, editor, consultant, and media personality, Norman has been a leading force in the world of lifestyle-related media for more than 25 years.

Introduction

It's a classic American dream: a beautiful log home nestled in the woods, standing proudly on a mountaintop, poised on a hillside, or serenely overlooking a sparkling lake or stream. With walls that beautifully blend the art of nature with the hand of human labor, no other kind of dwelling so poetically expresses the pioneering, self-sufficient spirit that made this nation great.

Since the 1970s, the appeal of log homes has escalated far beyond what one might ever have imagined. In the period between 1995 and 2001 alone, sales of log homes in the United States grew by almost 50 percent, according to a study by the Log Home Living Institute. "Living Like Lincoln," a November 21, 2004, article in *Time*, noted that Americans build more than twenty-five thousand log homes each year, representing more than 7 percent of the custom-home market.

The proliferation of "kit homes" is one of the reasons log homes have become popular. A kit home usually consists of not only the logs themselves but also the components used to put them together (such as spikes, gaskets, and splines) and install the windows and doors. Some kits even include specialized beams and lumber for roofing systems. Many such kits also arrive with blueprints and even a detailed construction manual to assist weekend builders who want to try constructing a log home on their own. Kits can run the whole ready-to-assemble spectrum from random-length logs to precut log kits to handcrafted homes made of large-diameter logs.

Of course, some ambitious individuals even decide to build their log homes from scratch, in some extreme cases even cutting down the trees themselves. Such approaches, however, are rife with potential short- and long-term problems, many stemming from the warping of improperly or insufficiently dried logs.

Another reason log homes, particularly kits, continue to grow in popularity is that they can be more energy efficient than homes created using more conventional construction materials and methods. A dried log is a naturally good insulating material composed of microscopic air pockets surrounded by sturdy cellulose fibers. Thick logs also have a significantly higher thermal mass than those of frame and drywall, so they keep interiors warmer in winter and cooler in summer, requiring homeowners to depend less on heating or air-conditioning systems. And walls of properly dried logs, when carefully constructed, are exceptionally weather-tight, also reducing heating or cooling expenses.

No matter what approach you wish to pursue, there are many things you must consider before attempting to purchase a log home kit or building materials. You must think about your lifestyle, the style of the home you want to build, your budget, and site selection. Additional concerns include choosing the right tree species, assembling the necessary building components, and planning for construction and long-term maintenance of your log home. You'll be more likely to achieve the home of your dreams if you consider each issue thoroughly. Most laypersons, and even many builders, are too inexperienced with log homes to make wise choices on their own—or even to know what issues to consider or questions to ask.

That's the reason for this book. Step by careful step, we will take you through the entire process as we've been doing for more than three decades.

One way to spark conversation around a campfire is to bring up the subjects of ghosts, snakes, or wood. We have heard many tales about all three topics. And, while we're not experts on ghosts or snakes, we do know a lot about wood.

Without getting overly technical, we have tried on the following pages to cover the basics, including drying, shrinkage, rot resistance, insulation, and fire resistance. We also discuss such important considerations as windows, doors, site preparation, log fasteners, gaskets, and log types. Our goal is to share the expertise we provide face-to-face and on the phone to our customers throughout the process of building a log home.

Based on many years in the business, we firmly believe that far too many potential customers do not have quality information available when they shop for log homes. This book provides you with that knowledge, enabling you to make intelligent decisions at every step of the process.

Knowledge will become your power when you deal with any log-home company. You'll become a smarter customer by learning how to select the right company, the right home design, and the right builder—and learning the right questions to ask and demands to make throughout the process. The result will be the log home of your dreams, a home you and your family will love and enjoy for many years—indeed, many generations—to come.

A Brief History of Log Homes

Early humans were essentially nomadic hunter-gatherers. They were on the move constantly to find sources of food and water. An occasional rock shelter gave them refuge from the weather and wild beasts. As they traveled, the best shelters they could make were animal skins placed over wooden frameworks, simply assembled structures that were light enough for the group to carry with them.

It wasn't until these early humans settled down to become farmers and herders that permanent dwellings became not only attractive but also necessary. Sound structures could not be built from logs or timbers until tools of bronze and, later, iron became available to cut and hew the logs. In the forested areas of what is now Europe, log dwellings were commonly built with the large amount of timber available. In the colder regions of northern Europe, these structures allowed the inhabitants to survive the winter.

Necessity and an abundance of trees also made log buildings attractive to early European settlers in North America, particularly to the Germans, Finns, and Swedes, who brought this technology with them to the New World. They squared their logs on two or four sides with an adze and then placed them one on top of the other with notched corners that made them sturdy enough to withstand the elements. A crude chinking of mud and moss sealed the logs when gaps opened between the individual rows. Thus, strong, weather-resistant (at least by their standards) homes could be constructed from readily available raw materials. They also included stone fireplaces for cooking and warmth, making use of the fuel that came from the same source of the homes themselves.

As pit saws and later water-powered sawmills came into existence, logs could be shaped to more exact dimensions than adzes allowed. Mills also produced lumber, and post-and-beam construction came into vogue. As the nation moved westward, the log home went with the pioneers. Log cabins were the housing mainstay of the West until sawmills produced lumber for towns and farms.

The first log-home boom began after the Revolutionary War and ended at the time of the Civil War. As the years went by, most of those early log homes were torn down or were covered on their exteriors with lumber, brick, or stone, which became America's preferred building materials well beyond the mid-twentieth century.

In the 1960s, however, another log-home boom of sorts came about when manufacturers started selling cabin logs and custom-designed log-home kits. These modern log homes showcased up-to-date improvements on tradition, including modern fasteners, windows, doors, and sealants to make weather-tight homes far beyond the dreams of our early ancestors.

In some of today's log homes, the richness of wood might be accented by lofty cathedral ceilings, lofts, and heavy-beam construction. They may contain all the amenities of an executive mansion, such as hot tubs, home theaters, and radiant floor heating. Indeed, many captains of industry build log homes as their private getaways!

Not all log homes have to be mansions, however. Many are small, weekend cabins, fulfilling their owners' long-held dreams to get back in touch with nature like America's earliest pioneers.

A log home isn't for everyone. But if you are reading this book, you are probably ready for a change from sheetrock and white paint—ready to carry on a tradition of building that has been around almost since the beginning of human history.

If you're seriously considering a log home, here are some questions you should ask yourself. Your answers can help you decide if a log home is right for you.

- **Money and location**: Have you completed the basic steps for buying/building a home, such as arranging financing, procuring a building site, and choosing a floor plan?
- **Region**: What part of the country do you live in? Are log homes common there and suited to the climate, terrain, and lifestyle?
- **Environment**: What environmental factors do you need to account for when building a log home? Is your region especially arid, humid, damp, dry, hot, or cold? Is a log home truly a good option in your region?
- **Size**: How big or small a home do you need? Will a log home meet your needs sufficiently?
- **Green living**: Is energy efficiency a major concern for you?
- **Building experience**: If you're planning to do some of the work yourself, do you have some experience in the construction trades?

- **Advance research**: Have you researched log homes? Are you familiar with the lifestyles they offer?
- **Finishes**: Have you made decisions about the type of wood you want and about the interior finishes, windows, and doors?
- **Direct experience**: Do you truly love the look and feel of a log home? Have you visited models or spent time in the log homes of others? Log homes have a definite "feel." For some folk, the rustic aura, however romantic it might seem, might be not be the right fit.
- **Maintenance**: Are you committed to the maintenance required to keep your log home in good shape? Can you do exterior treatments yourself, or can you afford to pay someone else to perform necessary chores such as sealing and caulking?

The Tree: A Wood-Producing Machine

Chapter Highlights

- As log home buyers, educating yourselves on the nitty-gritty details about wood and timber is smart.

- A tree is composed of the crown, roots, cambium, xylem, heartwood, phloem, and outer bark. All serve important functions in a tree's growth and lifespan.

This subject needs to be of prime interest to the log-home buyer because a log home requires a lot of wood. To build with wood, you must understand its positive and negative aspects. In this age of plastics and noncorrosive metals, many people have forgotten the basics of wood.

Don't let anyone start giving you overzealous claims about the wood used in their log packages. If it sounds too good to be true, it probably is. We have heard and read many stories over the years. A lumber mill said that its logs and lumber were cut from trees grown at a high elevation and thus were resistant to decay. Actually, the species of tree determines rot resistance, not where the tree is grown.

Some people think that locally procured wood will weather better in their area than logs or lumber from a region far away. This is not true. Weathering depends on the species of wood used in a home's construction.

One manufacturer claimed its logs were notched in such a way as to prevent longitudinal (lengthwise) shrinkage. Logs shrink only an infinitesimal amount in the longitudinal direction, so the notching has nothing to do with shrinkage. We have had people tell us about notching the corner logs in such a way that the notches get tighter when they shrink. We have yet to see such a notch. If wood wants to move, it will.

Another silly story came from someone who said that fence posts cut from trees in the winter have more rot resistance than those cut in the spring or summer. This tale probably comes from the idea that winter-cut wood is dry and summer-cut wood is wet. The fact is that winter-cut wood can have more, less, or the same moisture content as summer-cut wood. Thus, winter-cut wood can shrink the same as summer-cut wood.

If you have any reservations about what you are hearing from suppliers, or if you're not sure what you need to know about wood, call or write to the U.S. Forest Products Laboratory in Madison, Wisconsin. It offers many booklets and leaflets on wood and construction with wood. An educated shopper will end up with the best product, a product that best suits his or her needs.

Parts of a Tree

To understand a log home is to understand trees and the wood they produce. Trees come in various shapes and sizes, but all have the same basic structure: crown, roots, trunk, cambium, xylem, heartwood, inner bark, outer bark.

Crown

The crown consists of the leaves or needles and branches at the top of a tree that produce food. Chlorophyll facilitates photosynthesis and gives leaves their green color. Through photosynthesis, leaves use the sun's energy to convert carbon dioxide from the atmosphere and water and nutrients from the soil into sugar and oxygen. The sugar, the tree's food, is either used or stored in the branches, trunk, and roots. The oxygen is released into the atmosphere.

Roots

A tree's roots absorb water and nutrients from the soil, store sugar, and anchor the tree upright in the ground. Roots are both lateral and horizontal. Some trees have a tap root that reaches down as far as fifteen feet. Each root is covered with thousands of root hairs that make it easier to soak up water and dissolved minerals from the soil. If you ever transplant a tree to your property, be sure to protect these root hairs, as just a very short period of exposure to the dry ambient air will spell doom for your transplant. Root habits range from the large taproot of the black walnut to the shallow, spreading roots of the American elm.

Trunk

The trunk, or stem, of a tree supports the crown and gives the tree its shape and strength. The trunk consists of four layers of tissue that contain a network of tubes that run between the roots and the leaves and act as the central plumbing system for the tree. These tubes carry water and minerals up from the roots to the leaves, and they carry sugar down from the leaves to the branches, trunk, and roots.

Cambium

The cambium is a very thin layer of growing tissue that produces new cells, which become xylem (sapwood), phloem, or more cambium. Every growing season, a tree's cambium adds a new layer of xylem to its trunk, producing a visible growth ring in most trees.

Xylem

The xylem, or sapwood, comprises the youngest layers of wood and accounts for the annual rings that appear as concentric bands in the cross section of tree trunks from temperate climates. Its network of thick-walled cells brings water and nutrients from the roots through tubes inside of the trunk to the leaves and other parts of the tree. As the tree grows, xylem cells in the central portion of the tree become inactive, die, and form the tree's heartwood.

Heartwood

As a tree grows, older xylem cells, which reside in the center of the tree, die and become lifeless parts of a living tree system (much akin to human hair and fingernails). Heartwood lies at the center of the tree, where xylem cells eventually enter a state of perpetual dormancy because heartwood is filled with stored sugar, dyes, and oils. This heartwood, in many species, is a darker color and can be more resistant to decay and insect attack than the exterior portion of the tree (the sapwood). Heartwood cells add strength and structure to a tree with their tough, fibrous mass, which enables the tree to stand

Inner Bark

The inner bark, or phloem, which is found between the cambium and the outer bark, acts as a food supply line by carrying sap (sugar and nutrients dissolved in water) from the leaves to the rest of the tree.

Outer Bark

The trunk, branches, and twigs of the tree are covered with bark. The outer bark, which originates from phloem cells that have died and been shed outward, acts as a suit of armor protecting the tree from insects, disease, storms, and extreme temperatures. In certain species, the thick outer bark also protects the tree from fire.

Wood: Factors in Insulation and Shrinkage

Chapter Highlights

- Log homes have special factors to consider with insulation and shrinkage.

- R factor, thermal mass, moisture content, and shrinkage will all have an effect on your log home.

Having some basic knowledge about wood will help you make decisions while building a log home. A number of factors affect the quality, durability, and stability of the wood used in your log home. These include R factor, thermal mass, moisture content, EMC, and shrinkage. To understand how wood acts as an insulator, we first must understand how heat is transferred.

Heat Transfer

Heat transfers through the walls, windows, and roof of a home using a combination of conduction, convection, and radiation. Conduction is defined as heat transfer through a solid material by contact of one molecule to the next. Heat flows from the higher-temperature area to the lower-temperature area. On a hot day, heat from the exterior ambient air will be transferred through the glass window to the inside of the home by conduction.

Convection, the second type of heat transfer, is based upon the natural upward flow of warm air and downward flow of cool air. In a cold climate, heated indoor air rubs against the interior surface of the window glass. As the air cools, it becomes dense and drops to the floor. As this stream of air drops to the floor, more warm air rushes to take its place at the glass surface, and the process starts all over again. This cycle is called a convective loop.

Radiant transfer is the third type of heat transfer. Radiant transfer is the movement of heat from a warmer body to a cooler body through infrared energy waves. This radiation is the same as the heat emitted from a hot metal object. You can feel the heat without actually touching the hot object.

Air leakage is the final way that energy can be transferred into the home. It is the largest factor contributing to heat loss in a home. This is expressed as the equivalent volume in cubic feet of air passing through a square foot of area.

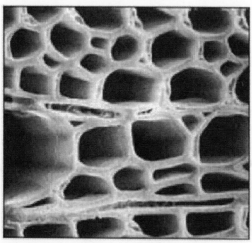

This microscopic photo of wood cells shows their porous structure. Photo courtesy of The Forest and Wood Products Research and Development Corporation (FWPRDC).

Thermal Resistance (R-Value)

Wood has value as an insulating material for three key reasons: its R-value, thermal mass, and weather-tightness. R-value (or R-factor) is a measure of resistance to heat gain or loss. The letter "R" stands for resistance. The higher the number, the better a product resists heat loss.

The major factor contributing to the high R-value of wood is the microscopic makeup of the wood itself. Air is a very good insulator. Gases like air do not transfer heat very well because their molecules are far apart from one another and greatly extend the time necessary for convective and conductive flow to occur. Dry wood happens to be composed of porous cells that hold air after the moisture has been removed. That is why the R-value, or thermal resistance of a building material, is calculated with a dry piece of wood as the baseline. If the R-value of wood was calculated from a green, unseasoned piece of wood, it would be significantly lower due to water's ability to transfer heat more effectively than air. The R factor is one criterion (if not the only one) used by building commissions to determine the energy efficiency of a conventional or log home.

Some mention should be made of the U-value, which is merely the reciprocal of the R-value. However, the R-value or U-value is not the true or only determinant of whether a home is going to be energy efficient. The other factors will be discussed in the following paragraphs. When calculating R-values, one must also consider the interior and exterior surface resistance of the log or building material. In the case of a roof, also figure in any air space, roofing felt, shingles, and decking on the roof and not just the insulation itself.

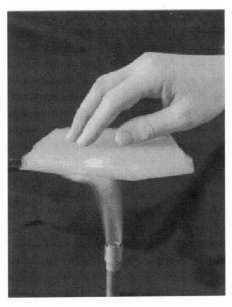

Aerogel, the world's lightest solid, has an R-value of 50 per inch. Photo courtesy of Aspen Aerogels.

Thermal Mass

In the past few decades, a second category of energy efficiency has become apparent in log homes. This is the effect called "thermal mass." Thermal mass is the ability of a material to absorb heat. Materials with high thermal masses operate much like thermal sponges or "heat sinks" because they cool a building during the summer by absorbing heat from the sun and releasing it over a period of time. When logs are heated in the winter, they tend to emit heat into the interior for a long time. This prevents the wild swings from warm to cold when the heating source is turned off. Larger logs have more mass than smaller logs and therefore contribute a larger positive thermal mass. Some companies give their products a higher R-value due to the materials' thermal mass. This is called "effective R-value" or "mass-enhanced R-value."

Our family had a large log home that was not heated on the weekends during the winter. One winter when the heat was turned on after several days, it took a number of hours to get the temperature up to a comfortable level. After the building was warm and the stove put heat into the building all day, the building was once again left without heat overnight. In the morning, it was much warmer than it had been the morning before, as the logs emitted the stored heat during the night.

Airtight Log Homes

The third factor in energy efficiency is how tightly the home is built. If there are gaps around windows and doors, around electric outlets, and between logs or exterior siding, then excessive air leakage can result, and the energy efficiency of the home can be compromised. Air tightness, however, should not be mistaken for insulation, and a well-insulated home should not be mistaken for an airtight home.

An airtight home offers many benefits, such as improved comfort by reducing drafts, noise, and moisture and improved indoor air quality by helping keep dust, pollen, car exhaust, and insects out of the home. An airtight home also reduces heating and cooling costs by preventing the escape of heated and air-conditioned air. In a 2000 article titled "Air Sealing – Bulding Envelope Improvement" (EPA 430-F-97-028) the Environmental Protection Agency estimates that air leakage accounts for between 25 percent and 40 percent of the energy used for heating and cooling in a typical residence.

In the past several decades, many systems have been developed that can check your home for air leakage problems. One test carried out by a large fan that puts a positive pressure inside the home tells the homeowner how much air is leaking out of the home by how quickly the pressure drops. Another test with infrared cameras can show hot spots where heat is leaving a building. Such tests are done after construction, however, and have no bearing on a home yet to be built.

Some engineering firms can work up a computer model to plan the energy efficiency of your proposed home. This will determine how the home should be sited and the most efficient location, size, and type of windows. Please see the discussion on creating an airtight log home in the construction section of the book.

Moisture in Wood Cells

The wood cells of a living tree are very porous and contain a great deal of water. In fact, the moisture content of wood in a tree can often exceed 100 percent. Moisture content, as defined in all aspects of timber production, uses the following formula: [(weight green − weight dry) / weight dry] x 100. In a live tree, there can be a greater weight of water than actual wood fiber.

Water is stored in wood in two main forms:

- Free water in the vessels or cells, which is used to move nutrients within the tree

- Cell (or bound) water, which is an integral part of the cell walls.

As soon as timber is cut, the wood starts to lose moisture. The initial reduction in moisture content is a result of free water loss. This usually occurs without any significant dimensional changes to the timber, as the loss of moisture represents the drainage of voids or vessels in the center of the cell. If the environmental conditions are favorable, the moisture loss continues until all free water is released from the cell lumen to the atmosphere. This point is known as the fiber saturation point (fsp). The fiber saturation point varies a little with each piece of timber or among species, but it is generally taken at a moisture content of approximately 30 percent.

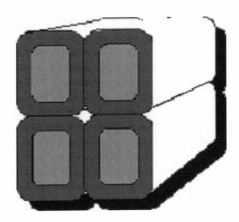

Moisture is contained in wood cells. Courtesy of FWPRDC.

The loss of free water will occur relatively quickly in small cross sections of timber, even if the timber is exposed to rain. However, in larger cross sections, free water can be lost over many months or years. Initial drying of the outside forms a hard "case," which can act as a barrier to further moisture loss.

After all free water has been lost, the timber will still contain moisture, but this moisture is bound into the cell walls. Much more energy is required to remove this moisture, as it is held in the wood structure by weak chemical bonds. This loss of moisture occurs more slowly than the loss of free water. It also results in a reduction in the size of the cell walls, which causes the timber to shrink .

When a timber or log has a great number of knots or large knots, degradation during the drying process can result. A large knot can make the timber bow in one direction or another, or the timber may not move at all. Even the location from which the wood is taken in the tree can make a difference. That is the fickle nature of wood. A log going from the green, unseasoned state to the dry state does not follow any standard rules. "Dry" doesn't mean zero percent moisture content but rather a percentage that closely approximates the equilibrium moisture content for the area in which the timber will be used.

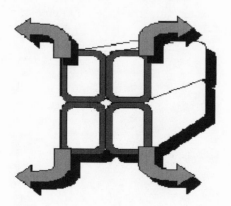

Moisture leaves the wood cells causing them to shrink. Courtesy of FWPRDC.

Moisture in Timber

Logs and lumber can only be shipped or used in one of two conditions: dry, seasoned wood or green, unseasoned wood. Unseasoned timber has a moisture content higher than the fiber saturation point (approximately 30 percent moisture content). In unseasoned timber, all of the bound water is present, and at least some of the free water is still in the wood. Unseasoned timber can feel wet to the touch. In some cases, if the wood is very green, water will drip out as a nail is driven in. This dramatizes an important point for log-home buyers: unseasoned wood is dimensionally unstable.

The moisture content of seasoned timber is 10 percent to 15 percent or less. The timber will lose very little additional moisture if used in a protected environment, such as under cover or indoors. The moisture content can vary depending on the geographical location in which it is used.

Partially dry or partly seasoned wood is not a substitute for wood that you are purchasing as dry material ready to be used in building a home. The wood will either shrink or not shrink. Shrinkage results when the wood transitions from the raw, freshly cut state to the dry state, which is at the equilibrium moisture content. Wood that does "not shrink" exhibits only small shrinkage when the wood goes from the humid summer months to the dry winter months (when the home is heated). Wood constantly gains or loses moisture through the various seasons as the humidity and temperature change.

Three steps are followed by people who know and use wood correctly:

1. Dry the wood to the moisture content that its end use dictates.

2. Keep the wood at that moisture content during construction.

3. Refer back to step one for each new piece of wood.

Equilibrium Moisture Content

Timber loses or gains moisture to keep in equilibrium with the atmospheric moisture in its immediate environment. When the timber and its environment have moisture contents in equilibrium, then the moisture content in the timber is known as the "equilibrium moisture content," or "EMC." No moisture will move in or out of the timber when the moisture in the timber is in equilibrium with the moisture in the atmosphere.

The actual value of the EMC of wood is mainly affected by the humidity and temperature of the environment in which it is being used. It varies a little with the species, but this is minor. Because moisture movement under normal moisture gradients is relatively slow, the annual average conditions of humidity and temperature are important. For instance, in Florida, where humidity is high, the EMC will be higher; in Arizona, where humidity is low, the EMC will be lower.

The EMC of timber used internally can be affected by the heating or cooling system for the building. Heating can dry timber more rapidly and depress the EMC. Air-conditioning also has a major effect on EMC, as the air is frequently very dry.

To minimize the movement of moisture into and out of the timber in service, it is good to have the timber close to the equilibrium moisture content when it is installed in the structure. This will reduce any adverse effects of further shrinkage or swelling of the timber.

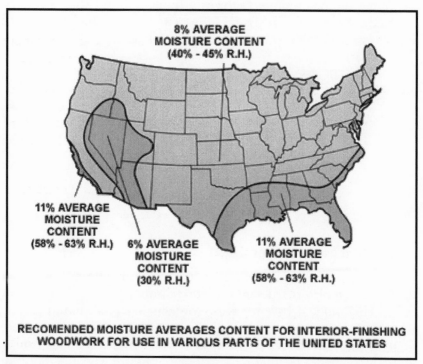

Recommended Moisture Averages in United States. Courtesy of the Forest Products Wood Handbook.

Shrinkage

As wood loses water and dries below its fiber saturation point, it shrinks. To prevent shrinkage and settling of logs, use dry wood, which has shrunk before milling.

Shrinkage is a reduction in the dimensions of timber due to the movement of moisture out of cell walls of the wood. Below the fiber saturation point, the remaining moisture is bound water and is an integral part of the cell walls. Removing this water causes small changes in the thickness of the cell walls. When this reduction happens to tens of thousands of cells, it causes reductions in the thickness of the timber or lumber.

There are three types of shrinkage:

- **Radial shrinkage** occurs perpendicular to the growth rings. It is shrinkage in the direction of the center of the tree.

- **Tangential shrinkage** occurs parallel to the growth rings. It is always a little greater than the shrinkage in the radial direction because radial shrinkage is partly restrained by rays (fibers that run perpendicular to the growth rings).

- **Longitudinal shrinkage** occurs when a board or timber shrinks lengthwise. Shrinkage in this direction is very small.

Shrinkage not only causes a change in cross-sectional dimensions but can also produce unsightly and sometimes dangerous splits and cracks that can often be avoided. In some cases, shrinkage can change load paths that may be potentially dangerous or costly to repair. That is why lumber gets its final grade only after drying and surfacing.

The effects of shrinkage vary depending upon the following factors:

- The species of wood

- The thickness of the timber or lumber

- The part of the tree from which the member was cut

- The initial moisture content of the material

- The rate of change of moisture and the environment in which the timber is placed

- The length of time the wood has been dried

- The method of drying the wood

- The part of the tree from which the material was cut

Shrinkage tends to be more of a problem for hardwoods than for softwoods. On ring-porous hardwoods, the ends of the lumber or timbers should be end-coated during drying to prevent excessive checking and splitting at the ends. This could be nothing more than several coats of paint, although special end-coatings are available and used by hardwood mills specializing in high-grade lumber to be either air or kiln dried. Regardless of the species, appropriate allowances for shrinkage need to be made in the detailing of all timber. The affects of shrinkage are obviously more significant for unseasoned timber allowed to dry in service. For some structural applications, using large cross sections of unseasoned timber may be necessary. These cases require careful design to limit the effects of shrinkage, particularly around connections where splitting or separation may occur.

The above factors of drying, milling, and cutting can enhance or decrease the value of the piece of wood. After the piece of wood is dried to a low moisture content, then it is milled into the final product. Any degrade that results from the drying process can then be discarded. We never know what a piece of wood will do in terms of degrade during the drying process. The drying process is an important wait-and-see procedure.

In a lumber mill, the log is sawed into lumber, sorted by size, dried, planed, and graded. Grading depends on a number of factors. The grading rules for lumber products are extensive and vary by species. Thus, oak is not graded in the same manner as pine; western red cedar is not graded the same as northern white cedar. Different associations—such as the Western Wood Products Association, the Southern Pine Inspection Bureau, and the Western Red Cedar Lumber Association—govern the grading of the various species of trees.

Snap, Crackle, Pop

Whether your logs and timbers were cut from dry wood or green (unseasoned) material, the wood will still go through some traumatic moisture changes when the heat is turned on inside the home during winter. Dry logs and timbers could have been rained on and picked up some moisture during the building process, and unseasoned timbers may not have lost enough moisture to bring them to the low EMC needed in a heated home.

For these reasons, we hear stories from homeowners about strange sounds coming from the log home when the heat is turned on in the fall and winter. These sounds are created when the heat from the furnace produces low humidity inside the home. The sudden heat and low humidity quickly dry and shrink the outer surface of the timbers, while the interior remains stable at a higher moisture content. This difference in shrinkage stresses the wood until—finally—a resounding "pop" is heard from the logs as the outer surface cracks open in a sudden release of energy.

Some homeowners understandably get the wrong impression that the home is falling down around them. These popping sounds are nothing to be concerned about, however, and can happen even if dry wood was used and the logs were constructed following the manufacturer's recommended procedure. Once the large timbers have reached their EMC, these snaps, crackles, and pops will diminish and then stop forever. Welcome to the world of log and timber construction.

Air Dried

The term "air drying" does not refer to leaving wood to dry in the air for a while. Air dried means that the wood has been dried to a moisture content that is in equilibrium with its environment. If lumber or timbers are air dried in a dry, arid environment, then the moisture content would be taken to a lower level than if they were dried in a humid, hot climate. I will point out a few examples. Florida has a humid environment. If wood dried in Florida has a moisture content of 17 percent, then it would be in equilibrium with the environment in the humid summer months. In Arizona, with its dry climate, this figure would be down around 10 percent moisture content.

To air dry lumber properly, it must be stacked so that air circulates around all surfaces of the material. The bark of logs must be removed before drying can commence properly. Strips of lathe-type material are usually used to keep the logs apart horizontally. Spaces are left between individual members in the vertical plane for proper stacking to facilitate drying. Covers should be placed over the stacks to prevent degrade from rain, snow, or sun.

If someone dries wood products in the air for a short duration (a few weeks or even a few months) and the moisture content has not reached EMC, then he or she cannot sell the wood as "air dried" to the consumer. The wood is still unseasoned. Consumers should be aware that truly air-dried lumber is stable.

There are many ways to tell if wood is dry, but to get a quick indication, just look at the timbers or logs. If they do not have seasoning checks or cracks, then they have not gone through the drying process to any extent. These cracks are caused by differential shrinkage. When a log or large timber begins to dry, the outside dries first and begins to shrink. The inside is still wet and does not shrink. Stresses build up between these two areas, and something has to give. This results in a crack. You cannot dry large timbers without getting some of these cracks in them. If you want the walls of your log home to look like paneling, then large-timber construction may not be for you. Before buying or building, look at some log homes to see if this is a look you like.

Kiln Dried

The kiln was developed to hasten and control the drying process so degrade could be kept to a minimum. Types of wood kilns include lumber, solar, and dehumidification kilns. To properly kiln dry lumber, the material must be properly stacked, stripped, and arranged in the kiln to allow uniform airflow around the bundles. Some companies have developed advanced three-dimensional airflow simulations to aid in kiln design and placement of the lumber within the kiln.

A kiln works by applying heat to the lumber. The heat is applied slowly at first and then more rapidly as the drying cycle commences. Humidity is controlled, as well as the heat, so that wood degradation can be kept to a minimum. These kiln-drying schedules are specific to the size and species of the wood.

The kiln does not change the nature of the wood. When it comes out of the kiln, the wood will resemble air-dried wood. Some people think that kiln-dried wood, which can be brittle, is lower in quality than air-dried wood. Others think that kiln-dried wood is stronger than air-dried wood, but this is not true if the moisture content for both air-dried and kiln-dried is the same. (When we talk of kiln-dried and air-dried material, we talk of properly handled and dried material not subjected to degrade.) Heat in the kiln can also destroy insects, insect larva, and fungus that may be on the material. Whether wood is air dried or kiln dried is not important. What is important is the final moisture content. If you are buying dry wood, you must know its moisture content whether the wood was kiln dried or air dried.

Kiln drying, as with other types of drying, must be carried out by competent workers, or the wood could degrade, resulting in a substandard product. When purchasing dry lumber or timbers, always look at the end product and get a written statement about the moisture content and the grade.

Tree Species Used in Log Homes

Chapter Highlights

- Your choice of tree species will have an impact on your log home in many ways: appearance, longevity, susceptibility to damage, and suitability for various elements of construction.

- Good information on various species will help you make the best choice for your log home.

Once you've selected a builder, supplier, or kit, you must determine which tree species will work best for you. Some customers tell us that a home built from locally grown trees is better, believing the wood will weather better than wood from trees grown in another part of the country. This is untrue. Weathering has nothing to do with the area in which the tree is grown.

For example, as a rule of thumb, pine is not highly decay resistant, whereas redwood, cedar, and cypress are highly decay resistant. Even though one species has a lower shrinkage factor than another, each should be dried (if a dry product is desired). Douglas fir and southern yellow pine have the strength characteristics appropriate for beams and timbers. Other pines, cedar, and spruce are not used for structural timbers. Southern yellow pines have a dark latewood, so the finished product has a nice appearance as far as grain and figure. Ponderosa pine appears yellow when aged, and the knots are dark brown or reddish. When a gloss urethane finish is applied, it has a very pleasing appearance.

Spruce and white pines are light in color and are stable in a wall or when drying. Aspen makes for a very attractive paneling due to its light color. Southern yellow pine, ponderosa pine, and Douglas fir are hard and can be used for flooring. However, you must realize that floors made of these woods are not as hard as floors made of oak or maple. Western red cedar, redwood, and spruce are soft and not suitable for flooring. Eastern red cedar has been used for flooring and is beautiful. The heartwood of the species is harder than most cedars and will stand up to average use. Decks should be constructed of cedar, redwood, or pressure-treated lumber. Western red cedar can be finished with a gloss varnish to bring out the grain and the red knots. Varnish should be reserved for interior use and not used on decks or the exterior of logs.

Table 1 shows a selected number of tree species from which timbers could be cut for wall logs and other portions of the log structure including rafters, joists, and paneling for interior walls. There may be others that have been used over the years, but they play a lesser role. If someone is offering logs or paneling from a species with which you are not familiar, consult your bookstore, library, or the U.S. Forest Products Laboratory in Madison, Wisconsin. Additional information about tree species appears in appendices A and B.

Hardwoods

The term "hardwood" designates broadleaf, usually deciduous trees such as oak, maple, ash, and elm. Hardwood trees produce a fruit or nut and generally go dormant in the winter. The term does not necessarily refer to the hardness of the wood. Hardwoods are of higher density and hardness in general, but actual wood hardness varies considerably; some hardwoods are softer than most softwoods.

America's temperate climates produce forests with hundreds of hardwood species, or trees that share certain biological characteristics. Although oak, maple, and cherry are hardwood trees, for example, they are different species. Together, hardwood species represent 40 percent of the trees in the United States.

Aspen (*Populus tremuloides*)

Aspen includes not only the quaking aspen but also the Bigtooth aspen. It is a hardwood but is softer than many softwoods. The wood is nearly white and is fairly lightweight when dry. Nails penetrate the wood easily due to its softness. If you are looking for wood that is rot resistant or has the strength required for rafters or joists, then you should not select aspen. It can be finished nicely on the interior of your home but will not stand up well to the weather.

A close-up photo of aspen trees. Photo courtesy of USDA Wildlife Division.

This species grows in the Rocky Mountains and the Great Lakes region, where it may be used as logs, but its main use is as paneling. It does make beautiful paneling, especially if you like a light-colored wood and are tired of knotty pine.

Red Oak (*Quercus rubra*)

The species *Quercus rubra* is part of the red oak group, which includes a dozen species. One species is about the same as another in terms of its use in construction. Generally, red oak is used in high-grade flooring or in furniture. The lower grades are used for pallets, boxes, and "dunnage," the little blocks of scrap stacking manufactured goods during transit. The FAS (firsts and seconds) grade is determined by how many clear (free of knots) cuttings can be obtained from a piece of lumber. Once selected for this grade, the wood is then kiln dried to a low, uniform moisture content, and the knots are cut out of the piece.

The heartwood is brown, and the sapwood is white. When first cut, it has an offensive odor, but this dissipates after proper drying for a long period of time. The wood is heavy and, due to its hardness, is hard to nail. Its density lowers the R-value of the wood. It shrinks significantly during the drying stage. It could be used for timbers for joists or rafters, but the length of beams is limited because most logs from oak are short. Large knots from limbs growing in the upper reaches of the tree can also limit its use, as with any timber, in a structural role. Remember, as with all woods, the grade must be matched with the final use.

Softwoods

Wood from conifers, trees that bear cones, is generally referred to as "softwood." The term is also used as an adjective for the trees that produce softwood. Softwood trees include pine, spruce, cedar, fir, larch, Douglas fir, hemlock, cypress, redwood, and yew. As the name suggests, the wood of softwoods is often, but not always, softer than that of hardwoods. Softwoods make up a far larger category of construction woods than hardwoods. This is due to their ease of nailing, their light weight, and the availability of sizes and grades. Thus, most conventional and log homes are built from woods in this category.

Bald cypress grows in the swamplands of the southeastern United States. Photo courtesy of Indiana Department of Natural Resources.

Tree species	Native geographic area	Color and appearance	Strength	Softness/Hardness	Suitability for structure	Suitability for exterior use	Suitability for interior use	Comments
Hardwoods								
Aspen	Rocky Mountains, Great Lakes states	White/light	Low	Soft	No	No	Yes	Good for paneling
Red oak	Not specified	Brown, can be knotty	Moderate	Hard	Limited	Yes	Yes	Generally used for flooring and furniture
Softwoods								
Cypress	Southeast	Yellow brown to dark brown	Moderate	Hard	Yes	Yes	Yes	Resistant to decay
Douglas fir	Northwest and Rocky Mountains	Reddish heartwood	High	Hard	Yes	Yes	Yes	Excellent for structural applications
Eastern white pine	Northeast and Great Lake states	White wood	Moderate	Soft	Yes	Yes	Yes	Soft wood resistant to twisting and warping
Lodge pole pine	Rocky Mountains	White wood	Moderate	Soft	Yes	Yes	Yes	A popular log-home wood in the western United States
Ponderosa pine	Western United States	Yellowish with red knots	Moderate	Moderate	Yes	Yes	Yes	An attractive wood with large red knots
Red pine	Great Lakes states and Northeast	Pale red to reddish brown	Moderate	Hard	Yes	Yes	Yes	The state tree of Minnesota
Southern yellow pine	Southeast	Yellowish wood	High, among the highest for all softwoods	Hard	Yes	Yes	Yes	The ability of southern pine to hold fasteners is among the highest of the softwoods
Western white pine	Northwestern United States and Rocky Mountains	Straight-grained, light-colored wood	Moderate	Soft	Yes	Yes	Yes	The state tree of Idaho

Tree species	Native geographic area	Color and appearance	Strength	Soft/ Hardness	Suitability for structure	Suitability for exterior use	Suitability for interior use	Comments
Eastern cedar	East	Dark red heartwood	Moderate	Hard	Yes	Yes	Yes	Good for furniture making and paneling
Western red cedar	Northwest United States and Canada	Rich red heartwood	Low	Soft	Yes	Yes	Yes	High R-factor, acoustic properties can provide sound insulation
Redwood	Northern California	Red heartwood	Low	Soft	Yes	Yes	Yes	Very resistant to decay
Engelmann spruce	Rocky Mountains	Light heartwood	Moderate	Soft	Yes	Yes	Yes	Widely used for log homes in the western United States
Northern white cedar	Great Lakes states and Northeast	White wood	Low	Soft	Yes	Yes	Yes	Popular for log homes, highly resistant to decay
Atlantic white cedar	East Coast from Maine to the Gulf Coast	White wood with light brown heartwood	Low	Soft	Yes	Yes	Yes	Heartwood is resistant to decay

Table 1: Tree Species and their Characteristics

Bald Cypress (*Taxodium distichum*)

This species is found in the Southeast from east Texas through Florida and into the South Atlantic states. Its availability has decreased over the years due to threats to its habitat.

The color of the heartwood varies widely. If you are interested in this species for use as logs or paneling, look at a large quantity of it in your supplier's yard to make sure that this is what you want. It can be light yellow-brown to chocolate brown to dark brownish red. The heartwood of this species is very resistant to decay. Thus, for decks and exteriors, it has always been a very attractive alternative to pine and fir. Cypress is used especially where wood will come in contact with moisture.

Douglas Fir (*Pseudotsuga menziessi*)

Douglas firs can be broken down into two main groups: the coastal Douglas fir and the Rocky Mountain Douglas fir (variety *glauca*). Another species, the big cone Douglas fir, is located in California, but it does not share the commercial impact of the other two species.

The coastal Douglas fir is used more than its cousin in the Rocky Mountains for graded, structural timbers. The coastal species has been cut from old-growth forests, so it has a high grade due to its high ratio of heartwood and lack of knots. The heartwood of fir is reddish, and the sapwood is white.

The species can be used for everything from dimensional lumber to timbers. In some areas, log-home manufacturers use this species for logs and, of course, beams, rafters, joists, and posts. In select structural wood, fir is a recommended species for rafters and loft joists. A structural engineer must size these timbers before you purchase them. The tangential shrinkage (7.6 percent from green to oven dry) of this fir is in the range of pine—it exhibits greater shrinkage than cypress, which we covered earlier.

Pine

Pines are coniferous trees of the genus *Pinus*, in the family Pinaceae. There are about 115 species of pine, and pines are the most important construction woods not only for log homes but also for plywood, dimension lumber, and boards. Pine is soft, easier to dry than denser woods, and found in abundance across the United States. Due to its softness, it is easy to saw, plane, mill, machine, and nail. It comes in a multitude of grades so that it can be used for furniture, pallets, beams, or trim. Its color and knot patterns lend a pleasing appearance to a final product that shows the wood pattern. Pine takes a stain or final finish well. The heartwood of some species can be somewhat resistant to decay, but it is best to avoid using pine where moisture can penetrate the wood. For exterior uses, such as decks, pine is pressure treated to prevent decay. Pressure-treated wood is not for interior use. In the following paragraphs, we will cover the most important pine species used in log homes.

Eastern White Pine (*Pinus strobus*)

Eastern white pine is the tallest tree in eastern North America. This species grows throughout the Great Lakes states, the Northeast, and down into northern Georgia. This species helped build the homes of America—from the first log cabins to the post-and-beam homes of New England to the homes and barns of the Midwest.

The sapwood is white, but the heartwood can be light brown. The wood is a straight grained, lightweight, and soft and easy to work with. The trees can grow tall and straight, so long timbers can be cut from the trees. Higher-grade wood can be used for millwork, and lower-grade wood for packing, pallets, and crates. It can also be used for knotty-pine paneling and for logs in a log home. Allow for shrinkage if you use green, unseasoned Eastern white pine, as the tangential shrinkage is 6.1 percent. Although it can be used for beams and structural members, this species is not known or marketed as a structural wood. It is mainly used for construction due to its ease in nailing and milling.

A stand of lodgepole pine trees.
Photo by Chris Schnept, courtesy of University of Idaho.

Lodgepole Pine (*Pinus contorta*)

The lodgepole pine was once used by native peoples to build tepees and lodges, hence its name. This is a species of the central Rocky

Mountains, although it also grows in Idaho, Montana, Oregon, and Washington. If you are building a log home in the Rocky Mountains, you will certainly hear of lodgepole pine. It is interesting to note that lodgepole pine cones often need exposure to high temperatures (such as from forest fires) to open and release their seeds

Much of the lodgepole pine harvested in the Rocky Mountains comes from "dead-standing" timber, which is discussed in the next chapter. Most of this wood has a light blue stain, but most Westerners think that this adds beauty and character to the final product. The timbers and lumber cut from these trees are fairly dry if the tree has been standing dead for a number of years and the bark has fallen off.

Lodgepole pine grows tall and straight, and long timbers can be sawed from mature trees. This species is not known for its strength for structural timbers or for its decay resistance, however. It is widely available in the Rocky Mountains and thus is widely used. When cut from mature trees—especially in its dry, dead-standing condition—it can be milled into high-quality house logs.

A forester checks a ponderosa pine. Photo courtesy of U.S. Forest Service.

Ponderosa Pine (*Pinus ponderosa*)

Ponderosa pine, named for its "ponderous" size, is one of America's abundant tree species, covering approximately twenty-seven million acres of land. It grows in Arizona and throughout the Rocky Mountains, as well as in the Black Hills of South Dakota and into California and Oregon. It is a yellow pine and contains more pitch than some of the other pines in the West.

Ponderosa pine is very pretty, with dark red knots that stand out against the yellow wood when a finish is applied. Due to the pitch, however, ponderosa pine can bow and twist, so this species is not known for its structural properties. When properly milled and installed, it can make a beautiful cabin log or paneling.

Red Pine (*Pinus resinosa*)

Red pine is a very old species, according to fossil records found in the Dakota sandstones in southern Minnesota. Red pine is also referred to as Norway pine. It grows in the northern parts of the Northeast and the Great Lakes region. The heartwood is darker than the sapwood and is pale red to reddish brown. In some areas, it is marketed along with the eastern white pine, as it grows in the same region.

Red pine is a hard pine that resembles the Southern yellow pine. The wood is moderately heavy, moderately soft, and moderately high in shock resistance. The wood has moderately large shrinkage.

This species is used for cabin logs mainly in the areas in which it grows. If you are building a log home in the Northeast or near the Great Lakes, you will hear of two building materials: eastern white pine and red pine.

Southern Yellow Pines

A number of species make up the broad category of southern pine. In the early part of the twentieth century, American home builders and farmers devastated the southern pine population and gave little thought to their use as a cash crop. They did come back, both in natural forests and on tree farms, and now make up a healthy part of the economy of the Southeast. These fast-growing trees are used for a variety of products. Though most commonly used as dimension and lumber, they have also been used in plywood and in pulp mills, which dot the Southeast. The pulp mills are especially important, as they can use trees thinned from forested areas as well as low-grade and defective trees.

The sapwood is yellowish white, and the heartwood is reddish brown. After some twenty years, the heartwood begins to form toward the center of the tree. In second-growth stands of southern pine, the growth rings can be very wide. Some species, especially longleaf and slash pine, are known for strength. The wood is hard and fairly heavy as compared to most softwoods. If properly seasoned, it is generally stable. However, we have found that it will bow and twist if not properly cared for on the jobsite while awaiting installation. In small timber with a large proportion of juvenile wood, this instability factor can be greater. Old-growth pine is much more stable than young, second growth.

Western White Pine (*Pinus monticola*)

The western white pine was named in 1831 by David Douglas, who was on a journey exploring the west coast of North America. It grows in southern British Columbia and Alberta down to northern California and Utah.

Large amounts of western white pine are cut in Idaho and Washington, and small amounts are harvested in western Montana and Oregon. Western white pine is a straight-grained wood that is cream to light reddish brown in color. It is easy to mill and very stable after proper seasoning. The wood is not known for its strength or for its resistance to decay. It has moderately large shrinkage from the green stage to the equilibrium moisture content.

Eastern Red Cedar (*Juniperus virginiana*)

Fruits on an eastern red cedar. Photo courtesy of U.S. Forest Service.

This species is more of a novelty in the log-home industry than a viable log material. It is known best by most people as aromatic cedar and is used for cedar chests and paneling in closets and dens. It is a beautiful wood. Much of the cedar timber is relatively small, however, so getting sufficient quantities of larger timbers (such as eight feet by eight feet or ten feet by ten feet) to manufacture house logs is difficult.

As mentioned, the wood is pretty, as the tree is made up of mainly blood-red heartwood. When properly milled, the dark red knots can enhance the beauty of the logs or lumber. This heartwood is highly impervious to decay and is resistant to insect attacks. Due to the large amount of heartwood filled with extractives, it has a low shrinkage factor. It is used for fence posts in many areas because of its decay resistance. This species grows, as the name suggests, in the eastern United States. In many areas, it comes into old, abandoned farmlands as a pioneer species, the first stage in reestablishing a forest.

Western Red Cedar (*Thuja plicata*)

This species of cedar is a completely different species from the eastern red cedar outlined above. They did not merely evolve in different parts of the United States. Western red cedar is found in the Pacific Northwest, Alaska, and western Canada. This species is sometimes called inland cedar when found in Idaho and Montana.

The heartwood of western red cedar is found in a wide variety of colors. It can be dark brown, pinkish brown, or reddish brown. This can all be found in the same bundle of cedar lumber. White streaks can appear in the wood as well. The sapwood is very white.

The wood is straight grained and mills very well. It has a pleasing fragrance when freshly cut or milled, but this soon fades, especially if a finish is applied over the wood. It is light weight and not strong, so it is not recommended for structural timbers. Due to its high rot resistance, it is often used for decks and railings. Due to its softness, the wood is better suited for interior paneling or roof decking than for flooring. It has a small shrinkage.

A man and his dog stand inside a giant redwood.
Photo by Paul Bolstad, courtesy of the University of Minnesota.

Redwood (*Sequoia sempervirens*)

This species is not a viable candidate for house logs due to its high price. Certainly, it is possible to mill logs from redwood, but it is not widely used for this purpose. Redwood is mainly used where rot resistance is a critical factor, such as for exterior decks and siding on buildings.

Engelmann Spruce (*Picea engelmannii*)

This species grows in the Rocky Mountains at higher elevations. It is a white wood with small knots. It is light weight and has a medium to fine texture. Because it is straight grained, it mills well with high-speed cutters. The Engelmann spruce is not known for its strength, so avoid using it for beams where strength is needed. The wood has a moderately small shrinkage, but that does not mean that it should be installed in the green, unseasoned state.

Northern White Cedar (*Thuja occidentalis*) and Atlantic White Cedar (*Chamaecyparis thyoides*)

We are joining these two cedars together even though they are different species because they are very similar. Northern white cedar grows in the northern part of the Great Lakes region over to Maine and down into the Appalachian Mountains. Atlantic white cedar grows from Maine down the Atlantic coast to northern Florida and as far west as the coast of Louisiana. Both species grow best in the swamps and bogs of their respective ranges. The sapwood is white, while the heartwood is light brown. The wood lacks strength and shock resistance. The heartwood is very resistant to decay, but the sapwood is not. The wood also has a fairly low coefficient of shrinkage and is soft and light weight.

Understanding the basics of various tree species will help you choose a tree for your log home and maintain your home after construction.

Timber: Logging and Preparation

Chapter Highlights

- Obtaining timber for your log home can be accomplished by professional logging or do-it-yourself methods.

- Once selected, timber must be milled and prepped prior to use in construction.

- Log types include cants, random length, precut, and handcrafted.

- Log profiles include round, flat/round, square, hand peeled, laminated, log siding, and siding with false corners. All have various issues to consider when building.

A logging truck hauls off a load in the early 1900s.
Photo by Brian Nelson, courtesy of Federal Motor Trucks Collection.

Professional Logging

Logging is the practice of cutting down trees and then cutting out their central boles (the clear trunks or central stems) and possibly branches in order to use the wood directly or to market the wood as an economic resource. Standing trees viewed as potential economic resources are termed "timber."

Loggers

Many people, known collectively as loggers, work in the forest to harvest trees. Fallers are the people actually cutting the trees. Next, choker-setters fasten chokers (steel cables or chains) around logs to be skidded (dragged) by tractors or forwarded by a cable system or skidder to the landing or deck area. The logs are then separated by species and type of product, such as pulpwood, saw-logs, or veneer logs, and loaded onto trucks. The job of a choker-setter is very dangerous and is usually the first job that a logger will obtain on a logging crew. Log sorters, markers, truckers, and debarkers sort, mark, and transport logs based on species, size, and ownership and tend machines that debark logs.

In the western United States, trees are harvested as "dead-standing" timber. Dead-standing timber is normally found in two species, Engelmann spruce and lodgepole pine, but also in ponderosa pine. Insects kill large tracts of timber. Once dead, the timber dries in its natural upright position. Either a private landowner or a government agency (in many cases, the U.S. Forest Service) will sell this dead timber to sawmills as a salvage cut. It is then sawed into lumber or other wood products. The advantage is that the wood is already dry or partially dry when it is used. How long it was standing dead in the forest will determine its dryness.

We mention this category of lumber because for many decades dead-standing timber has been used in log-home construction throughout the western United States. Countless log homes have been built from dead-standing timber with excellent results.

Helicopter Logging

CH-54 Skycrane hard at work. Photo courtesy of Erickson Air-Crane.

A discussion of logging today would not be complete without mention of a helicopter logging site. Helicopter logging is being used in response to the growing environmental concerns about traditional logging methods. On a helicopter site, the timber is felled in the conventional manner, but instead of being transported to the landing with a skidder or cable system, the logs are connected to a skyhook hanging beneath a helicopter and flown to the landing. This minimizes ground disturbance.

The drawback of such a logging method is the high cost. The operating cost of a helicopter such as the Erickson Skycrane can run up to five-thousand dollars per hour. Obviously, with this sort of an hourly cost, all other operations are designed to maximize production during the flying time. Chokers are preset to create turns that will provide a load for the helicopter but not overload it. When multiple logs are needed to make up the weight, they are strung end to end. This way, the helicopter can lift them off the ground using a Skycrane equipped with onboard scales attached to the drop line and a quick-release hook. With helicopters dropping off logs rapidly, the landing area can turn into a pile of logs and chokers very quickly. Time is money when the operating costs are nearly a hundred dollars a minute.

Clear-cutting

The method of timber harvesting is generally used in the West, where large stands of mature timber are found. Taking some of these mature trees and leaving the rest does not make sense, as they are all in the autumn of their lives and need to be harvested. Many mature stands grow very slowly, are overcrowded, and have rot. Thus, it is time to take out the complete stand and start over with a new stand of timber.

These stands generally contain species that require full sunlight to propagate and flourish, and a new stand cannot readily come in under the shade of trees left in the stand. When the land is cleared, the bare soil and full sunlight will allow the propagation of a new forest. Nature has been doing essentially the same thing for eons; forest fires, hurricanes, and high winds take out the old timber, and a new forest comes in. Selective thinning of young stands is done in the West so that the remaining trees can prosper. This, however, is not the case with large, mature stands.

In many of the forests across the United States, selective cutting is still employed. Large, mature trees are removed to make room for the trees that remain.

Logging Your Own Timber

The least expensive but most labor intensive way to build a log home, in terms of initial outlay, would be to cut the trees from your own land if suitable trees grow on your property. This requires a chain saw, a tractor or skidder to pull the logs from the woods, and a truck to haul these logs to your building site or to a sawmill, where the logs can be sawed into some usable form.

Logging is one of the most dangerous occupations in the United States, if not the world. If you are unskilled in dropping trees with a chainsaw or in pulling them from the woods, a warning should be sounding in your head. Building a log home by cutting your own trees is only suitable for a professional woodsman; it is not for the uninitiated. Be sure to have plenty of insurance if you attempt this, because you may very well need it.

Over the years, we have heard countless stories of people who have tried to build a home in this way. The end results have not been good. Many people tell us that they want to build their log homes from trees growing on their lands, but they have no idea of the difficulties in this endeavor. These neophytes head off into the sunset to cut their trees, but I seldom hear from them again. More and more counties and states have strict building codes, so this method of construction is becoming more limited. They just won't let you harvest trees from your property unless many structural and safety codes are met, so think again before considering this approach to building your log home.

The Sawmill

After timber is cut, it must be processed before it can be used in construction. From hand-cut logs to water-powered and steam-powered mills, the early days of processing cut timber was hard work. The work is still hard, but in the twentieth century, the introduction of electricity and new technology has advanced this process. Today, most sawmills are massive, extremely expensive facilities, and almost every aspect of the work is computerized. A modern mill can produce millions of board feet of lumber per year.

To get this product to market without a long holding time, dry kilns dry the lumber quickly. The lumber is planed to the customer's specifications, and then it is shipped to wholesalers. Most of the material placed in the dry kiln is dimension stock (such as two-by-four feet through two-by-twelve feet) or one-inch lumber to be planed into various patterns for use as interior trim and paneling.

Types of Logs

Cants

When the logs reach the sawmill, they are cut into boards or cants. Most log-home materials start off as cants. A cant is a log that has been squared on two or more sides. The pieces cut off the log to make the square cant are called slabs. Cants can be nothing more than logs with slabs cut off the top and bottom giving a uniform surface on which to stack succeeding courses of logs. They could also have three sides slabbed so that the inside of the home will be flat. Finally, all four sides of the log can be sawed to end up with a fairly uniform cant. Although you will seldom find log homes built from four-sided, square cants, they do exist. In some areas of the country, people refer to these homes as "tie houses" because they look as if they were built from railroad ties. (A note of caution: Do not attempt to build any structure from old railroad ties or from any pressure-treated wood. This has been done in the past, but the pressure-treated chemicals contained in the wood can cause severe health problems in humans.)

Cants stacked and ready for milling at a sawmill. Photo by the authors.

You can take your logs and have them custom sawed at a local sawmill, or you can buy cants directly from the sawmill. In either case, the bark must be peeled off the cants, and then the cants are stacked with an inch of space between each cant and each row, which allows air to circulate around the unseasoned material. Without air, the wood cannot dry. A cover is placed on top of each stack of cants to prevent the rain and snow from wetting them periodically. In humid areas, a fungicide should be sprayed on the logs to keep them bright and to prevent them from mold and fungus. Closing up the cants in a barn, where outside air cannot freely circulate, is also not a good idea; they will not dry properly and will become infected with mold and sap stain.

The most beneficial aspect of sawmill cants over rough, round logs is that they will be easier to join, especially if they are three-sided cants. They will also be fairly uniform, which will aid in construction. To make them even easier to use, they should be run through a planer on the top and bottom so they will be uniform in their stack height, and, in turn, you will have walls of uniform height on which to build the trusses or rafters. This operation should be done after the drying process is complete. A rough, sawmill cant is a first-generation-type log.

Using cants to build a home can be beneficial, but it also has drawbacks. A higher degree of skill is required to build with this type of log than with the milled log. Although large homes are built this way, for the do-it-yourself builder, cants are best relegated to the small hunting cabin. Always know your skill level, and don't overestimate what you can actually do. Before beginning any type of log-home construction, find out what construction materials and methods the local building commission allows. As mentioned before, never leave a structural engineer out of your building equation.

Random-Length Logs

In some areas of the country, you can purchase milled logs in various lengths—mainly between eight and sixteen feet. A single or double tongue and groove (T&G) may be milled into the top and bottom surfaces of the logs. Random-length logs are milled accurately with a planer or lathe, so you don't have to contend with logs of different dimensions. Like milled lumber, milled logs stack evenly because each log has a uniform height. Most random-length logs on the market are uniform in width, so log walls can be built up straight and plumb using guide braces. Placing rafters and ceiling joists is much easier when the walls are constructed this way. Remember to adhere to the exact dimensions on the blueprints, and do not change the prints while you are building—it can come back to haunt you at a later stage in the construction process.

When purchasing random-length logs, you should ask some important questions:

- **Dried or green?** Are the logs dried, or are they green, unseasoned logs? Dry logs weigh less than green, unseasoned logs. They are also more stable in terms of shrinkage, twisting, bowing, warping, and cracking. If you are buying dry, seasoned logs, get the moisture content stated on the sales receipt.

- **Instructions?** If the logs are purchased unseasoned, get instructions on how to construct the walls to allow for any shrinkage or settling.

- **Cut square?** Are the logs cut square at both ends so that they will need minimal cutting and trimming?

- **Pre-drilling?** Will the company pre-drill the logs for the spikes or lag screws? If so, you will save time by not having to do this procedure on the job site during construction.

- **Graded logs?** Are the logs mill run or graded? Grading can be done from an aesthetic point of view where cracks, barky edges, and rot are thrown out, or it can be done according to specific grading rules. If the latter, a certified lumber inspector grades the logs. A grade stamp appears on the end of each certified log. However, logs graded by a lumber inspector might meet grading standards but have defects that you deem unsightly. Ask the supplier to state the grade of its logs in writing.

- **Species?** From what species of wood are these logs milled? Some species are better for construction than others. Refer to the section of this book on wood to learn more about the different species of trees used for construction, specifically for wall logs.

- **Guarantee?** Is there any kind of guarantee if the logs are not what you ordered? What if you receive a different configuration than you wanted? What is the company's policy if you ordered dry logs but your logs are still unseasoned when they arrive? Check these policies carefully.

- **Quantity check?** When your material arrives or when you pick it up at the manufacturer's yard, count the items so you have no questions later.

We do not mean to scare you from proceeding with your plan to build a log home, but you should be educated when purchasing logs. Be a wise shopper, and pay attention to detail so that you can make the construction process pleasurable. There are many reputable companies that supply logs, lumber, and materials for the log-home builder. When you pay attention to detail, you also help the supplier give you exactly what you want.

When someone has trouble purchasing materials, the supplier or contractor is not always at fault; the homeowner's lack of understanding of logs and log homes may contribute to the problem. You should not be your own general contractor if you are not versed in construction. This is a much more complicated profession than most people think.

Precut Logs

Two stacked "D" logs. Photo by the authors.

Many companies that offer kit homes also offer precut log packages. The packages may consist of precut logs only or include precut rafters, log gable ends, and second-floor beam joists. Although precut logs offer some advantages to the do-it-yourself builder, they can have hidden drawbacks.

When the log-home company delivers these precut log structures, it will provide a detailed "log plan" to show where each log goes in the structure. This results in minimal if any cutting and fitting of the logs. Thus, the builder picks up the correct log, puts it into the proper position in the wall, and secures it to the log below. Presto! It's just like putting together the toy logs that many of us played with as children. Right? Wrong.

The logs are heavy, and expertise is required not only to anchor them securely but also to make sure that no gaps remain at butt joints and at corner joints. You must remember to place the gasket and caulk as required by the supplier before securing the log and not after. If you set the wrong log in the wrong place, or if a log moves during the spiking process, then you lose valuable time ripping out the log and doing it correctly. On-site technical assistance from the manufacturer is useful. We recommend that you hire experienced log builders to help you for a few days so you will not make mistakes that are hard to fix later.

With random-length logs, the builder can adjust the next cut to cover an error made earlier. With a precut log package, the builder must adhere to specifications on the blueprints. If the builder deviates from these specifications, problems will result later in the building process. If the home is thirty-two feet by forty-eight feet, then the logs must be laid to these exact specifications. If the wall is not built plumb as the logs go up, then gaps will begin to appear at the butt-and-corner joints.

The precut package offers the advantage of going up faster on the job site; saving time can mean saving money or getting your home shelled in before the winter snows or spring rains. Also, joints will be tighter because the logs are cut square in the supplier's plant. Consider for a moment the expertise required to cut a large log square without a cutting table.

Cutting through large logs requires a specialized saw. If you think you can just grab a chainsaw and begin cutting logs to length without any type of guide, you are mistaken and will produce a substandard wall. A chainsaw is fine for cutting firewood, but it leaves a splintered face on wall logs. With a precut package, the window and door openings are already cut out, so you don't have to figure out where each window and door will be located. (In the above discourse, we are referring to the do-it-yourself builder. A competent log builder can use random-length logs without the problems encountered by a first-time homebuilder.)

When the rafters and the log gable ends are also precut, the builder must get the log walls up according to the blueprint specifications. If the walls are not plumb, the rafters and/or gable ends will have to be recut and custom fit. If this is not done by someone with a great deal of expertise, the log courses could contain gaps due to improper fitting on the job site.

Lastly, on a precut log home, the logs must be separated and sorted by log number before the first log is put in place. This may take a number of hours or a whole day, depending on the size of the home. But it must be done so that the home can be built in a systematic manner. If this is not done and a log cannot be found, the first thing that builders may do is call the manufacturer and report "missing" logs, or they may cut the first log they see to the length they need. Now they have definitely set themselves up for missing logs during the construction phase. If a sixteen-foot log is cut into a shorter log, the shorter log cannot be used when the longer log is finally needed. Haste makes waste! If you select a precut kit, you should have construction knowledge or find a knowledgeable builder to do the work. Building a home takes expertise; if you forget this, you will waste a lot of time and money.

When buying a precut log package, there are a number of questions to ask the supplier:

- **Dried or green?** Are the logs dried, or are they unseasoned? If unseasoned, you will need to address several issues during the construction phase, including slip joints on window jambs, openings over windows and doors for shrinkage and settling, screw jacks to accommodate settling in the home, and so on.
- **Species?** What species of wood will be provided?
- **Cut tolerances?** To what tolerances are the logs cut: plus or minus one-sixteenth inch or one-half inch?
- **What's precut?** Just what is precut in the log package—the logs only? Or are rafters, joists, and gable ends also precut to fit the specifications of the house?
- **Predrilled?** Are the logs predrilled for the spikes and/or lag screws?
- **Outlet cuts?** Are the electrical outlets cut into the logs? Beware on this one. Codes vary from state to state, and problems result if outlets do not meet local electrical codes when the building inspector arrives. This is also an area of concern if the electrical outlets have to be cut on the job site. Spacing between outlets and height above the floor are governed by local building codes. Check with your local building inspector before installing electrical outlets.
- **Extras?** Are extra logs provided in case a log is damaged during construction or if a log is missing on the job site?
- **Construction manual?** Is a detailed construction manual provided so the logs can go up in a timely fashion?
- **Window and door cutouts?** Are window and door openings cut out so this doesn't have to be done on the job site?
- **Log layout sheet?** Will the supplier give you a copy of the log layout sheet prior to delivery so you can see what logs are provided and if the right window and door sizes

are incorporated? Most companies will have you sign off on this sheet to ensure no misunderstandings prior to the home being cut.

- **Package contents?** What is included in the package—windows, doors, gasket, spikes, lag screws? What kind and brand of windows and doors are included?
- **Will the supplier provide the answers to these questions in writing on the invoice?** This is a must.

The precut home will go up more easily with accurate cuts at the butt-and-corner joints, which will result in a nicer-looking home, if the manufacturer has diligently prepared the kit. However, as with all log packages or with logs in general, you must follow all specifications and make accurate measurements. Don't let anyone tell you that the whole inexperienced family can go out on weekends and build a log home as a fun and easy endeavor with great savings in construction costs.

Handcrafted logs

Handcrafted log kits are another variation of the precut log kit. These kits utilize large logs in the range of twelve to twenty-four inches in diameter, usually hand peeled, and contain all of the charm and variation of raw logs. A select group of people prefer the massive logs and the look reminiscent of lodges found in the western mountains or the palatial homes once built in the Adirondacks of upper New York. The logs do not come in one standard diameter or configuration but rather vary in diameter and taper. The logs are hand hewn at the mill to fit at corners and joints and at the horizontal surface so the log above fits the log below to avoid large gaps. Joints are sealed with gasket or caulk or both. This type of log most closely resembles the logs used by our forefathers in the early United States, especially in the West, where large trees (and thus logs) provided the only building material prior to the establishment of sawmills.

The manufacturer of handcrafted logs utilizes many skilled craftsmen to cut and fit each log at the factory. The total log package is fitted and built at the factory prior to disassembly and numbering of the components. When the logs arrive, a crane is normally needed to lift each precut and numbered component into its proper place; the sealant is placed as the walls go up. The time on the job site is kept to a minimum because skilled builders erect the log package, and heavy equipment swings the logs, joists, rafters, and gable logs into place.

A handcrafted home is more expensive than one built from a log kit due to the large size of the timbers, the many months of labor needed to cut and fit each log by skilled craftsmen, and the freight costs to deliver these logs to the job site. Normally, these homes are built for individuals with a love for the real log-lodge look. Such logs are not usually cut for the small, inexpensive, seasonal hunting or fishing cabin. Handcrafted homes are built to the custom design of the discriminating homeowner, for whom cost is not a primary factor. When completed, they are awe-inspiring in their size, their lofty cathedral ceilings, large supporting beams, and purlins.

The usual concerns and questions pertaining to the precut log package also pertain to the handcrafted log home. Some concerns and questions for manufacturers are:

- Do they do custom designs?
- Do they provide a building crew, and is this included in the basic price of the kit?
- What are the transportation charges?
- Are there labor charges?
- What are the shrinkage/settling allowances?
- Do they have a turnkey (ready to use) option with their builders?
- What is included in the cost?
- Does the price include the logs, the construction of the kit, and the drying of the wood?
- Are there any turnkey costs from previous homes?

If you think that this is the home for you, ask some manufacturers about the types of logs they offer and the required lead time and request an estimated price per square foot for the package and completed home. They should have a range of figures for past completed homes. This will be just a range of figures, as no two homes are alike. Ask questions, and then decide if a package is right for you. Needless to say, doing groundwork and asking many questions are the hallmarks of any good buyer of a log package.

Types of logs	Advantages	Disadvantages	Ease of use	Limitations	Comments
Cants	Low cost and readily available	High skill level needed	Low	Best for small projects (i.e., cabins)	Quality can vary considerably
Random-length logs	Low cost	Must be cut to length on job site	Medium	Time-consuming for the novice	Can make changes while home is being constructed
Precut logs	No cutting required	No changes can be made during construction	High	Logs must be sorted before use	Must be assembled properly
Handcrafted kits	Have already been assembled at factory	High cost	Low	Skilled carpenters are required for this type of construction	Crane may be required for assembly

Table 2: Log Types

Log Profiles

Round Logs

Round logs consist of timbers turned nearly or completely round. They are joined on the top and bottom with a tongue-and-groove system or with a Swedish cope. At the corners, some type of saddle-notched corner is used.

Some people like this completely round log because they feel it provides a rustic look resembling the log cabins built throughout the West in the nineteenth century. They also think that a log building should be round on the inside to give their home "the real log look." The saddle-notched corners also appeal to these buyers. Keep in mind that the round, interior surface of this profile can collector dust, a problem of any log with a protruding face. Such homes are also a little harder to construct because the interior stud walls must be notched into the round face of the log. And although the logs may be nine to twelve inches in diameter at the widest point, they are much narrower at the point where one log sits on another. In some states,

Round log profile with Swedish cope.
Photo by the authors.

this smaller log width can be considered the thickness of the wall in energy calculations. Although the energy actually lost through this narrow area is open to speculation, you should check with the building commission prior to deciding on a log package. We have known homeowners who were very pleased with the overall energy efficiency of this style of log home, even though their homes were built with eight-inch-diameter round logs in cold, mountain climates! In fact, we have not heard any complaints from homeowners on the energy efficiency of this type of log.

If you are thinking about round logs, or any log for that matter, check the local building requirements for log thickness, R-value, windows, and roof insulation. In some areas, you can increase your roof insulation to offset a log of marginal size. First, check the regulations and codes in your area, and then decide if this is the log style for you.

Flat/Round Logs ("D" Logs)

Some log-home enthusiasts like the flat interior of the "D" log, which will give the interior wall a look of paneling. Log homes that utilize this style normally use the butt-and-pass system of joining the logs at the corners, but you can do a saddle-notched corner. A single or double tongue and groove in the top and bottom of each log allows a tight seal between each row of logs.

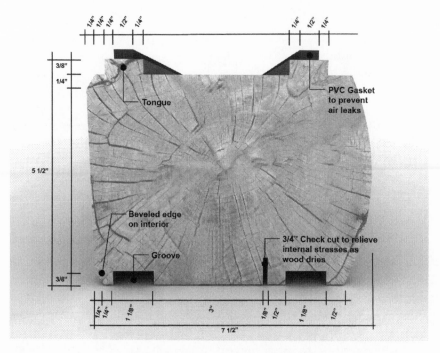

Anatomy of a "D" Log. Photo by the authors.

A drip edge may be milled into the lower exterior edge of the logs, allowing a driving rain to drip from the logs without seeping between them. A bevel (V-joint) is milled at the top and bottom edge of the interior face of each log, giving a more pleasing effect than one continuous, flat face on the interior of the log wall.

Square Logs

A log style that has found favor with some clients is the square, timber-type log, which is flat on the interior and exterior. This style of log is also normally built with the dovetailed corners found in log homes once built in the Appalachians.

The logs can have a tongue-and-groove sealing system on the top and bottom (the horizontal surfaces) as with the more common "D" log, or they can use a different sealing system completely. A popular sealing system uses a piece of rigid insulation between each course of logs; this rigid insulation may be two to four inches thick. After the log walls are completely erected, a wide strip of chinking is applied over this insulation and between each row of logs. This is done on both the exterior and the interior of the home and gives the home the old-fashioned, mountain-cabin look of years gone by. Many manufacturers have their own methods of sealing the logs and cutting the corners, however. If you're interested in this type of log, check out the various manufacturers who specialize in a square log with dovetailed corners.

To give a more rustic look to the interior and exterior faces of the log, the log can be hewed by hand with an adze. For this type of home, the corners could also be tied together using a half-lap or even a corner post. With corner posts, the logs butt into the posts, giving a neat appearance. If the corner post is used, the log/post connection must be adequately sealed and attached with lag screws.

Hand-Peeled Logs

A number of log-home manufacturers use logs that are round on one or two sides, with the round surfaces hand-peeled to lend a rustic appearance to the log. To seal the logs, the tops and bottoms are milled with a tongue and groove, or a spline system is used. When the natural logs are left round on the interior and exterior walls, the diameters of the logs in the wall will vary. For instance, if a nine-inch log sits on a ten-inch log, a ledge forms. To prevent rain or snow from collecting on these exterior ledges and causing moisture problems, the home design must include large overhangs (a good idea for any home). With this more rustic log, notching the interior stud walls into the exterior log walls may require additional construction time.

Many people like the rustic appearance of this type of log; the trade-off is price. Freshly cut logs should always be provided for this type of home. If you see bark falling off the logs or sawdust coming out of holes bored by insects, beware!

Although the butt-and-pass system is probably the most common, a number of different corners can be used. Check if the company can also provide log gable ends as well as log rafters and second-floor joists. All of these will help bring together a rustic log home that will look the same throughout.

Laminated Logs

A special category of logs is manufactured from dimensional lumber. For instance, five two-by-eights are glued together, forming a large timber. This timber is then run through a large planer to cut a tongue and groove into the top and bottom. The interior and exterior are milled with the normal round/round, round/flat, or flat/flat configuration. Some companies can even furnish a log with an interior face of pine and an exterior face of western red cedar or other species. Many combinations are available, so you need to talk about the options with the manufacturer.

The lumber that makes up such a log must be high grade, kiln dried to a low, uniform moisture content, and milled smooth prior to gluing. If any one of these steps is skipped, then a lower-grade product will result. Thus, you should buy from a company that has the expertise and equipment to do the manufacturing properly.

The advantages are that the log is dry, made from high-grade material, free of any seasoning cracks that often appear in large timbers, strong, and very stable. Some people do not like these logs, however, because they consider them to be manufactured logs and not true, solid logs. Also, some do not like the appearance of the laminating at the ends of the logs. There is always the chance that delamination will occur if the log is not properly maintained.

Laminated log. Photo by the authors.

With any home, periodic maintenance is important. If the homeowner does not perform maintenance in a timely manner, the exterior components, including windows and doors, will degrade long before their normal lifespan. If you have not cared for your log home as recommended by the manufacturer or as dictated by common sense, do not blame the supplier of the logs when problems develop.

Log Siding

Although log siding does not consist of real logs, it is used often enough in construction to warrant its inclusion here. Log siding can be used to construct a new home or to reface an existing home. It can be purchased in a number of different species, but pine and spruce are common.

There isn't any mystery in using log siding in a home: just build a conventional home, and use log siding on the exterior in lieu of metal, vinyl, or brick. You must know proper installation procedures in detail. Do not dive into the process without knowing what to do; this can result in the siding not stacking up uniformly and problems later due to warping or decay. The log siding normally comes in 2×6 or 2×8 sizes. Larger sizes are available from some manufacturers, but these two sizes make up the bulk of what is sold. In both cases, however, the actual milled sizes and styles can vary greatly. Be sure to order plenty so you will not run short of material. The supplier can help you determine the amount of log siding needed for a particular job. Many people are confused by measurements such as board

Log siding.
Photo by the authors.

feet, linear feet, and square feet. By purchasing the correct amount of material, you will not have to special order and wait for a small quantity later.

Log siding commonly uses one of two systems to seal each row to the one below: a ship-lapped system or a tongue-and-groove system. Of course, some siding does not use either method—especially rustic siding, which has some or all of the bark on it and may not have a sealing system milled into each edge. Siding using the tongue-and-groove system may be a harder to fit together if any boards are twisted or warping, but it can be "blind nailed" so that the nails (or screws) are not visible. Some builders may still want to "face nail" periodically so that the siding will not come loose as it is subjected to the vicissitudes of nature. With ship-lapped log siding, one nail is blind nailed into the top tongue portion of the lumber, and another is face nailed on the lower side of the lumber.

With any siding that does not have a sealing system milled into it, one must rely on caulk or chinking to seal the horizontal seam. Using this type of material for any exterior application is not wise, as rain can get behind the siding and cause moisture problems.

Siding should be thoroughly kiln dried or air dried before use. The moisture content should be below 15 percent for best results. Kiln-dried log siding will have a grade stamp on one side. The normal grades for this type of lumber are "No. 2," "No. 2 or better," or "No. 3." A "No. 3" grade will have more knots or more bark on the edges than a "No. 2"grade. Grades will vary widely by species and by grading agency. For instance, in western red cedar, you may want siding that is kiln dried, select, tight knot, or a "No. 2" grade. Always check for missing or loose knots in the lumber, and watch for rotten knots in some species. If you find a lot of missing or loose knots, then you will accumulate a lot of waste or have problems with the knots falling out later. For air-dried log siding, be sure that the supplier states the grade and the moisture content.

Do not leave the log siding lying around the job site for several weeks before installation. This will result in bowing or warping of the material, which cannot be blamed on the manufacturer or supplier of the product. Keep your log siding in the bundle and under cover, and use it promptly.

With all exterior lumber, use galvanized nails or plated deck screws to attach the log siding to the stud wall. If regular nails or screws are used, a black stain will appear when rain comes in contact with the siding. This will then bleed down the siding, resulting in an unsightly appearance.

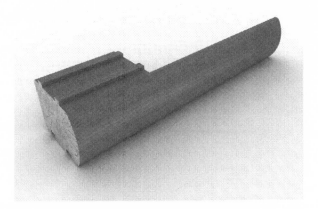

Example of a false corner. Photo by the authors.

Some companies offer log-siding products that have matching false-log corners. Such a corner has a short log stub at one end and a longer return that matches the log siding. The stub may be eight to ten inches long, and the return that matches the log siding would be sixteen and thirty-two inches. This return, which joins to the log siding, allows the joints to be staggered at the corner of the building. By being sixteen and thirty-two inches long, they will end on a stud so that they can be nailed securely. These specifications may vary from manufacturer to manufacturer.

By using this system, one can build a conventional frame and cover it with siding and false-log corners to give the look of an authentic log home. When properly constructed, a log siding façade can look like real log construction. Log siding can also be used on buildings that are already constructed but whose conventional siding has seen better days and needs refacing.

A note of caution: if a building that needs refacing with log siding has very marginal overhangs, we would think again before refacing with wood. The marginal overhangs can allow water to run down the log siding with every rain and increase maintenance problems. Also, the sun will give it a severe beating, and you may be throwing "good money after bad" by trying to resurrect an older, poorly designed building with real wood. In such cases, vinyl or aluminum siding would be a better choice. Log siding is an option, however, especially with new construction. For best results, follow the guidelines for roof overhangs and the other construction tips to follow.

Log Corner Sections

Butt-and-Pass Corners

The butt-and-pass corner is probably the most widely used corner section for log homes. Alternating logs protrude from the exterior, which gives a stair-step effect. This is widely used with 'D' logs, which are flat on the interior of the home. Carefully consider the length of the overhang. Some builders construct overhangs of sixteen inches, whereas eight inches is a much better length. If the log protrudes too far, it will collect rain and snow, which can lead to decay. These unsupported logs can also twist over time as the sun beats down on them. Thus, we recommend the eight-inch overhang.

Example of the butt-and-pass corner system. Photo by the authors.

Saddle-Notched Corners

This type of corner is widely used on logs, such as Swedish coped logs, that are turned round on a machine. It is also used on handcrafted log homes when the logs have various diameters. The overhanging logs are even on the ends. Some people prefer this style, as it resembles the log homes built in the West in the past.

Example of the saddle-notched corners. Photo by the authors.

Dovetailed Corners

This corner is used on square logs such as eight-by-twelves, which are reminiscent of the homes built in the Appalachian Mountains in the 18th and 19th centuries. A special dovetailed notch is used, and the logs are even on the ends. These logs are chinked, in many cases, to give the look of days gone by.

Example of a dovetail-corner system. Photo by the authors.

Windows and Doors

Chapter Highlights

- Your choice of windows and doors impacts your log home's appearance, durability, and energy efficiency.

- Different window styles and construction methods have advantages and disadvantages.

- When choosing doors, both interior and exterior, consider your needs for security and privacy, sound, and weatherproofing.

The subject of windows and doors could fill a book in itself. Manufacturers in the United States offer extensive and diverse lines of products. Yet, many people who set out to build or improve a home don't have a clue about what type of windows and doors to install. This chapter aims to highlight some basic facts that apply to all windows and doors. For more information particular window and door manufacturers and their products, read the ads and articles in popular consumer magazines, or visit the companies' Web sites.

When deciding what type of window to put into your home, you will need to balance cost with energy efficiency. Energy-efficient windows will cost more up front but will bring you long-term savings on heating and air-conditioning. You will also have to match the right type of window to its particular end use. You wouldn't want to put a large window in a bathroom, for instance, or a small window in a bedroom with a private view.

Energy Efficiency

A window is a potential site of significant heat transfer and can not only contribute to problems in maintaining a comfortable environment within your home but also raise your heating and cooling bills. To combat these problems, the glazing industry has come up with several innovations to improve thermal insulation. To help us select the most energy-efficient windows, we must first understand how windows transfer energy.

Heat Transfer

As mentioned in the chapter "Wood: Factors in Shrinkage and Insulation," heat is transferred from an object in three different ways: conduction, convection, and radiation. Windows primarily transfer heat by radiation. When you sit in front of a glass window during a cold winter day, the long-wave radiation from your body passes through the window. The window acts as a heat sink and takes heat from your body. This is why you feel cold sitting in front of a large window even though your home is heated.

Air leakage is the largest factor contributing to heat loss in a home. The pressure difference between the outside and inside of the house causes air to flow around the sash and through the frame of a window. Most windows come with an air-leakage rating (AL), which is expressed as the equivalent cubic feet of air passing through a square foot of window area. The lower the AL, the less air will pass through cracks in the window assembly.

Window efficiency is expressed with five different measurements: R-value (or R-factor), U-value (or U-factor), solar heat gain coefficient (SHGC), emissivity (E), and visible transmission (VT). As discussed in a previous chapter, R-value is a measure of resistance to heat gain or loss. A product with a high R-value resists heat loss well. U-value, the reciprocal of R-value, is the measure of the rate of heat loss through a material. The lower the U-value, the greater a window's resistance to heat flow and the better its insulating value. Look for windows with low U-values and high R-values. A window with a low U-value keeps heat in during cold days and keeps heat out during hot days. The larger your home's heating bill, the more important a low U-value becomes.

Solar heat gain coefficient measures how well a window blocks heat from sunlight. The SHGC is the fraction of the heat from the sun that enters through a window. SHGC is expressed as a number between zero and one. A window with a low SHGC transmits little solar heat.

Emissivity is a measure of the amount of heat emitted from an object by radiation. We will learn about low-E windows in the next section.

VT is an optical property that indicates the amount of visible light transmitted through a window. Windows with high VT are easy to see through and admit lots of natural daylight into a home. Some tints and coatings can reduce visible transmission. The VT range in residential windows extends from a shady 15 percent (a VT value of 0.15) for some tinted glass up to 90 percent (a VT value of 0.9) for clear glass. Windows with VT values above 0.6 look clear, while windows with a value below 0.5 begin to look dark and/or reflective.

Energy Efficient Solutions

Insulated Glass

Insulated glazing units (IGUs), or insulating glass units, are two or more panes of glass spaced and hermetically sealed to form a single unit with a gas-filled region between the panes. The gas between the panes ranges from low-cost dehydrated air to expensive inert gases such as argon or krypton, which provide better insulation. Some companies manufacture triple-glazed windows, which use three separate panes of glass with room air or another gas between the panes. When using IGUs in high-elevation areas, a breather tube must be installed into the window. If this breather tube is not in place at high elevations, the glass can break due to the pressure difference between the glass panes. This difference in air pressure occurs because most windows are manufactured at lower elevations, where air pressure is greater.

Low-Conductance Spacers

Layers of glass found in IGUs are held apart by spacers. In the past, window spacers were made out of aluminum, but due to the highly conductive nature of metals, these proved to be ineffective. Many window makers now offer a product called a warm-edge spacer. These spacers are made from less conductive materials like thin stainless steel, plastic, foam, and rubber. Warm-edge spacers can improve the U-value of an entire window unit by 10 percent. In addition to being a barrier to heat flow, spacers prevent moisture from entering the sealed cavity.

Tinted Glass

Tinted glass and tinted window films have long been used in commercial buildings to reduce heat gain through windows. Lightly tinted windows are becoming more common for the residential market in southern, cooling-dominated climates. These new glazings reduce the solar heat gain without reducing visibility as much as older tinted glass and films.

Low E

Coated glass is typically called "low E," or low emissivity. The coating is composed of an extremely thin layer of metallic oxide that reflects up to 90 percent of long-wave heat energy (radiation) while passing shorter wave, visible light. Some coatings will also screen out ultraviolet light, preventing your drapes and carpet from fading

Frames

The material used to manufacture the frame has a major impact on the thermal characteristics of the window. Because the frame represents 10 to 30 percent of the total area of the window unit, frame properties influence the total window performance. Window frames are made from a range of materials including aluminum, wood, vinyl, and fiberglass. Composite window frames are also common.

Metal frames are generally poor energy performers because metal is a good conductor of heat on clad windows. Homes in warm areas of the southern United States use inexpensive aluminum windows because heating concerns are not as critical as in northern climates. In northern climates, interior moisture will condense on the cold, interior aluminum surface, causing the window to "sweat." You can order metal frames in the color of your choice, however, so you do not need to prime and paint the windows after installation.

Windows can also be purchased with a primed exterior coat over the wood trim so that the final paint scheme can be applied. This is laborious and must be redone periodically. The bottom line is that they will sell for somewhat less per unit than clad windows, and the buyer is able to save money via "sweat equity."

Unprimed, bare wood exteriors are available from some manufacturers. Some home purchasers like to leave a natural exterior by using a clear coating or to stain the trim to match their log home. The downside is the labor this entails. The elements can damage your windows if they are not touched up periodically. If you like the natural look, be prepared for this periodic maintenance schedule.

The Future

Every year, the window-manufacturing industry makes great strides in developing new products that just a few years ago would have seemed like science fiction. One of the latest such developments is the transition-metal switchable mirror.

Transition-metal switchable mirrors, or TMSMs, are glass panels with a coating capable of switching back and forth on demand between a transparent state and a reflective one. TMSMs save energy because they both reflect infrared light and manage interior levels of visible light by allowing daylight to pass to the interior when available. When the sun is bright, TMSMs switch to a highly reflective state, cooling the inside of the home; in low light conditions (during cloudy periods or at dawn or in the evening), TMSMs switch to a transparent state, allowing daylight and heat to enter and warm the home.

In the long run, these expensive but highly energy-efficient windows are worth the cost, considering that windows are weak spots in a home's total insulating efficiency. Your local window dealer or log-kit supplier can give you more specifics on the merits of cost versus increased energy efficiency. A smart buyer will always do the research first, of course, to find the window that best suits his or her situation.

Recommended Window Properties				
Climate Zone	U-Value	Solar Heat Gain Coefficient	Visible Transmission	Air Leakage
Northern	0.35 or less	<0.55	>0.50	0.30 cfm/ft^2
Central	0.40 or less	>0.55	>0.50	0.30 cfm/ft^2
Southern	0.65 or less	>0.40	>0.60	0.30 cfm/ft^2

Types of Windows

Many styles of windows are on the market. From the most expensive to the least expensive, they include operable casements, awning, gliders, double-hung windows, single-hung windows, and fixed picture windows. A bay window, which is less expensive than a bow window, is made up of fixed glass in the center with either casements or double-hung windows on the sides.

Casement

Casement windows have a handle on the inside that you crank to open the window for ventilation. If you are choosing a single window, the manufacturer will need to know if you want a left-hand or a right-hand swing. This depends on the direction of your prevailing wind. Double windows have a left-hand and a right-hand swing. Triple units usually have a left and a right swing on the sides and a fixed window in the center.

The casement window is an airtight unit. When cranked shut and locked in place, it provides a very tight seal. These windows are highly recommended for windy locations, but they are the most expensive. We do not recommend casements on a deck or porch, because someone (a child especially) might run into the window when it is swung out in the open position.

Because the casement window swings out for ventilation, the screen is on the inside of the window. For triple glazing, a storm panel can be applied to the interior of casement windows for added insulation. Such a measure is recommended at northern latitudes on the north or northwest side of a home. And, of course, high-performance glass contributes to the energy-efficiency of the home.

Casement window. Photo courtesy of the authors.

Double-hung

The double-hung window is made with two moveable sashes, one on top and one on the bottom. These slide up and down independently of each other. When in the closed position, they can be locked with a sash lock. Most quality window manufacturers make these windows so that the sash can be removed from the inside of the home. The tilt, take-out window can be released from the sash liners to facilitate cleaning, which is especially helpful if the window is on the second story of your home. Check out this feature and see if you can remove the sash by yourself at the sales office. The way the sash is removed varies by manufacturer.

Because the double-hung window is made of two sashes, air may leak where one sash meets the other and joins the sash liner. In windy areas, a home benefits from a triple-glazed window utilizing a storm window on the exterior. In most cases, this storm window is a combination unit with a sliding glass portion and a screen for summer ventilation. This is not the storm window from days of yore that we took out of storage from the garage in the fall and installed for the winter and then removed again in the spring. These combination storm windows can stay on year-round.

The double-hung window is a trade-off between price and energy efficiency. We do not want to give the impression that the double-hung window is a bad choice; the casement window, however, is a tighter window. Most homes in the United States are fitted with double-hung windows. If you have an unlimited budget, you can buy the very best of everything for your home, but most home builders do not have unlimited funds. You must make decisions and trade-offs based on your budget.

Double-hung window. Photo courtesy of the authors.

Single-hung

In a single-hung window, the bottom sash moves, and the top sash is fixed. This window is not a popular, and manufacturers have limited inventories, if they carry them at all. We would not consider them for a home, but we might place them in the garage to save a few dollars. They are less expensive because only one sash moves.

Glider or Sliding

This type of window is basically a double-hung window on its side. Some people find gliding windows easier to open than "crank-outs," such as casements and awnings. Some people may install this window over a hot tub for ventilation, but not extending down to the tub area. You can achieve a high degree of light and ventilation by placing the window above the floor. This specialty window is for specific a purpose and is not as widely used as casement or double-hung windows.

Awning

Awning windows are hinged at the top and open outward. The awning window is used for ventilation. In many great rooms, awning windows are placed at the bottom or top of a fixed glass window for ventilation. They are also used in bathrooms and above hot tubs to provide ventilation, but the windows are positioned high for privacy.

Bay

Bay windows are combinations of three or more windows projecting outward from a room. Bay windows come in many heights and widths. These windows are generally used in a great room or master bedroom and fitted with a window seat for potted plants or knickknacks. To accommodate this window seat, a bay window protrudes from the wall of the home. Bay windows can be obtained in either a thirty-degree or forty-five-degree angle, where the flanking windows meet the fixed glass in the center. They allow a lot of light into the room and have a pleasing appearance from the outside.

The center glass makes up the bulk of the unit, with either operable casements or double-hung windows located on either side of the fixed window to allow for ventilation. A bay window costs more than a fixed-glass picture window but less than a bow window.

Picture

A picture window can be merely a pane of fixed glass (the most inexpensive) or a pane of fixed glass in the center flanked by an operable casement or double-hung windows on either side. The picture window is flat and does not protrude like a bay or bow window. A picture window with the flanking operable windows is less expensive than either a bay or bow.

Bow

Bow windows are made up of a number of casement or double-hung windows and form one large curve. They are more expensive than picture or bay windows, but they give a home a contemporary look. This may or may not be the look that you want on your log home. Quite frankly, we see many more bay and picture windows installed in log homes. As we have said many times, it all depends on one's taste.

Bow window. Photo courtesy of the authors.

Greenhouse

A greenhouse window is a three-dimensional window that projects from the exterior wall and usually has glazing on all sides except the bottom, which serves as a shelf. A greenhouse window is a specialty window that is often used over sinks. The greater amount of light will allow plants to be placed in the window for a nice touch. A variety of sizes and designs are available, so ask about them when purchasing your windows.

Specialty Windows

Windows can be designed to meet any criteria. Just keep in mind that when we talk of special-purpose windows, the price tends to go up. If you are on a budget, don't waste the window supplier's time by asking for a lot of specialty windows. Take the less expensive route first; if the price of your home is less than you expect, you can add a few specialty windows (or doors).

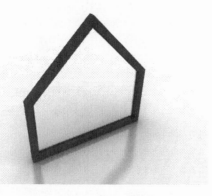

Specialty window. Photo courtesy of the authors.

Arched windows (also called circle-head windows) or elliptical windows add nice touches over dormer windows or over a patio door. They also look pleasing at the front of the home. Be sure that you have enough wall height if you are going to add circle heads over large windows. Adding another course of logs might be prudent so that you don't crowd the ceiling or second floor of the home.

Round and Octagon

These specialty windows have been used to good effect in bathrooms or on the sides of shed dormers to allow a little more light into the loft area. They can be a little hard to install into a log wall as opposed to a stud wall in the dormer or gable end area. They come in a variety of sizes and can be either fixed or operable. An operable window is more expensive than a fixed window.

Angled Gable

In the gable ends, many people like a lot of glass to allow light to come into the home and to provide a good view of the landscape. You must match the glass with the glass in the patio doors or large, fixed-glass panels on the lower level of the gable end of the home. One way this is accomplished is by using glass shaped like a triangle, trapezoid, pentagon, or rectangle.

If you decide on angled glass, the angle must match the pitch of the roof. This is the reason that most window companies do not want you to order this glass until the roof is on your home and the rough openings are framed out. Your builder will then give the window salesperson the actual measurements, and the company will manufacture the windows to fit this rough opening.

These windows should be ordered with the same exterior finish as found on the rest of your windows. With large glass areas, use the high performance, low-E glass to increase energy efficiency. Don't skimp on budget here, or you will pay more in the following years.

Stained Glass

A custom piece of stained glass placed in a gable end or bathroom will compliment any home. Stained glass can be custom ordered from a local purveyor. The stained glass can be installed on the inside of the home, and a glass panel can be installed on the exterior to protect the stained glass from the elements. This window can be the centerpiece of your great room, kitchen, or hot-tub area.

You can also ask your supplier if etched glass is available. This can add a pleasing effect to circle-head windows located over double-hung or casement windows.

Because windows are not as energy efficient as the log wall, you must balance light, cost, and energy efficiency. Putting a lot of glass on the north side of your home, for example, is bound to raise your heating bill and drain your wallet over the years due to the cold winds coming from this direction. Installing very large areas of high-efficiency glass can also raise your heating bill in the winter. Additionally, the sunlight that pours through can add to your air-conditioning costs during the summer.

To determine the best mix of log and glass, meet with an architectural firm and generate a computer model of your home and site. This is much better than just selecting a window style because you think it might look good.

Doors

Doors fit into two broad but obvious categories: interior and exterior. Most log-home kit suppliers do not provide the interior doors, so we will cover a few facts about the m.

Double-light entry door. Photo by the authors.

In the average home, the entry door is a 3/0 by 6/8 door. This means that it is three feet wide and six feet, eight inches tall. The rough opening for a pre-hung 3/0 door is normally three feet, two-and-a-half inches wide by six feet, ten-and-a-half inches tall.

The bathroom door is a small 2/4 in width, and the bedroom is a little larger at 2/8. You could use a 2/6 width for the bathroom or the utility room. We are tired of trying to get hutches, dressers, or couches through small 2/8 doors, so in my home, I would have 3/0 doors throughout. How much more does that cost? Not much. Also, in the planning phase, try to locate doors so that you won't have to angle a dresser at 45 or 90 degrees to get it into a room. These are small points, but small points pay off if enough of them are incorporated into the floor plan.

What is the difference between a left-hand and a right-hand door? This is a question that comes up all the time. The answer involves the swing of the door. Do you want the door to swing in to the left or in to the right? A left-hand door swings in to the left when you are facing the door from the outside, and the doorknob is on the right. A right-hand door swings in to the right, and the doorknob is on the left. Although most doors are ordered as "in-swing" doors (they swing into the room), they can be ordered as "out-swing" doors, particularly if you do not want the door to hit against furniture in the home. Ask a salesperson what options are available.

Doors can be purchased in many designs, construction types, and materials. Hollow-core doors are the least expensive on the market and are damaged easily. Two pieces of thin veneer make up this door, and the core is hollow.

A much-preferred door for the interior of a log home is the solid door manufactured from pine or fir. This is a quality door that will not only take punishment over the years but also add to the pleasing décor of your log home.

Of course, a myriad of custom doors are on the market, and your budget will dictate what you can place into the rooms of your home. By researching home-improvement or decorating magazines or the Web, you can find many manufacturers of these magnificent custom doors to meet your discriminating taste.

Exterior Doors

Most entry doors are usually 3/0 by 6/8. If they come in a kit, they should be pre-hung so that they will fit into the proper rough opening allowed for in the logs. Most entry doors that come with a standard kit have glass on the top and solid wood on the bottom. The rear door

French doors. Photo by the authors.

may be solid, especially if it faces north. When pre-hung, they should be weather stripped and have an adjustable sill. The manufacturer should provide the proper jamb extender to fit the thickness of the logs and bore the holes for the door lock(s).

Ask your supplier for help in selecting a door that fits the décor of your home. Do not simply pick the most expensive doors, which may have etched glass or special configurations in the glass that add to the cost. For extra light, sidelights (normally twelve or fourteen inches wide) can be added to one or both sides of the entry door.

In years past, the solid wood door was available to the buying public. It was made of real wood and looked expensive. Today, the insulated steel and fiberglass doors are taking over the market for exterior doors. These doors come pre-hung, just like the solid wood door, but they have several advantages.

A metal or fiberglass door will not warp like a solid wood door, even if it is left to the mercy of the elements. In our many years in the business of manufacturing log homes, we have seen very few solid wood doors warp. These were generally not finished or maintained properly and had gotten wet. The insulated door is more energy efficient and less expensive than the solid wood door. The steel door has one disadvantage over the fiberglass door. If a heavy blow is leveled against the steel door, a dent can result. With the fiberglass door, this dent will pop out again after the pressure is relieved from the blow or kick.

Many people like insulated doors, as they can be painted to the same color as the metal roof or the window and door trim. Of course, wood doors can be painted as well, but they are normally left natural so that the grain of the wood can be appreciated.

With all doors, a double bore ensures that a regular door lock with handle and a dead-bolt lock can be fitted. These two locks, and all of your locks, should be keyed alike so that you don't require a whole pocket of keys to unlock the various doors of your home.

When buying a kit, look over the manufacturer's literature on doors (and windows) to see what options are available. Don't be content to stick with the door in the package. Ask about the manufacturer's guarantee on its product(s).

Patio Doors

A multitude of types, sizes, and configurations of patio doors is available. As with windows, you need to look over the product literature carefully. If you are building your dream house, then you take time to select the door or doors that you want. We will discuss two types of patio doors: sliding-glass doors and swinging doors.

Sliding-Glass Doors

The sliding-glass door is an attempt to combine windows with a door so that plenty of light can enter the home. The normal size is 6/0 by 6/8. Other common widths are 5/0, 8/0, 9/0, and even 12/0. The height can be obtained in the normal 6/8 but is also available in 6/5 and 8/0. For more light and style, a transom can be installed on the top of a patio doors. This transom could be in the shape of a circle head, referring to window units with one or more curved frame members, or an eyebrow. The eyebrow design does not take up as much height above the door as a circle head.

The sliding-glass door is less expensive than other patio doors such as swinging French doors. The sliding-glass door does not have a door leaf that swings into the room, so furniture can be arranged closer to the door without obstructing passage through it. It probably isn't as good for security, as we have seen people remove a door panel when locked out of their homes. Only one panel moves, creating a large opening for furniture and other items is impossible. If dirt, gravel, or foreign objects get into the track, then the door will not slide properly. This is especially true if snow gets into the track, melts, and then refreezes at night. Finally, sliding-glass doors are not as weather-tight as swinging patio doors.

Swinging Patio Doors

This popular group of doors has many trade names and is manufactured by many companies. Like sliding patio doors, swinging patio doors come in many sizes, both in width and height. You can also order a glass transom for the top of the door.

The door is usually an "in-swing," but an "out-swing" door can be obtained as well. An array of swing combinations can also be obtained. On the most popular sizes, like the 6/0 by 6/8, either the right or the left panel can swing. For those who desire a large opening at some time or another, both panels can swing. This may be desirable if the door leads to a deck and would facilitate the flow of traffic from the deck to the kitchen or from the deck to the family room. A patio door with two in-swinging doors requires a double-hinged screen, adding to the price of the unit. If you purchase a 9/0 or 12/0 size, then a greater number of combinations of operable and fixed panels are available for the door unit.

For a large area, we suggest high-performance glass. You definitely notice the difference during the life of the home. Many door locks and styles are available, and we suggest installing a deadbolt. Swinging patio doors close tightly and are thus more energy efficient than sliding patio doors, especially in high-wind areas. They get their energy efficiency just as the casement window—by shutting tightly with minimum air leakage.

The companies manufacturing the patio door offer many color options for the exterior cladding. Of course, the primed-wood swinging patio door is also available, and some companies offer the unprimed, natural-wood finish for those wanting to stain the exterior of the woodwork.

Keeping It Together: Fastening and Sealing Methods

Chapter Highlights

- Fasteners are crucial in log-home construction. Avoiding gaps is important to energy efficiency and maintenance.

- Sealing your log home will have long-term effects on its durability, energy efficiency, longevity, and appearance.

Fasteners

The subject of fasteners is very important in log-home construction. If the wrong fastener is used, gaps could appear between the logs, letting in water and air. Walls can lose their structural integrity without proper fastening.

A number of fasteners for attaching logs to the log wall are on the market. Kit manufacturers have different ideas about what is best for their logs. If you are in doubt about the fasteners used by your log-home supplier, ask a structural engineer's opinion. You also need to ask an engineer about the spacing of the spikes or screws used to attach the logs to one another. In seismic or high-wind areas, log fasteners and spacing will have to be upgraded for structural integrity.

Spikes

Spikes look like standard nails but are much larger. Their lengths are usually eight, ten, twelve, or fourteen inches. They come in two fairly common diameters: three-eighths inch or five-sixteenths inch. The three-eighths-inch spike is most common, as it is less likely to bend when driven into a large log or when it hits a knot. The smaller spikes will give you more spikes per fifty-pound box, and when used in cedar or spruce, they are less likely to bend—unless a sledgehammer delivers a glancing blow. Always wear eye protection and gloves to protect yourself from splinters of steel dislodged from the spike.

Spikes can come in either smooth or spiral configurations. The spiral spike will hold better than the smooth, but if you ever need to pull up a log, it will be very difficult with the spiral. Spikes come in either the regular steel finish or a galvanized finish. Galvanized spikes are recommended for unseasoned logs that contain a lot of moisture or for logs contain tannic acid or other extractives.

Logs should be predrilled before spiking. Predrilling is done only on the log being spiked—not on the one below. This lessens the labor required to pound each spike into the log. Always pound the spike head well below the top of the log so that the head will not hold the logs apart and prevent a tight seal. Always pound the head of the spike down securely so that you obtain maximum holding power. Check with the manufacturer of the log kit for specifics on fastener sizes and lengths. When in doubt, ask a structural engineer.

Lag Screws

Most professional log-home builders favor using lag screws to secure logs, rafters, and joists. This is due to their greater holding power when compared to spikes and their ease of use. Lag screws can be secured in place with a heavy-duty electric drill or an impact tool. First-time home builders usually favor the electric drill. Place a socket adapter, which can be obtained at a well-stocked home center, in the drill. This adapter will have a nine-sixteenths-inch socket head that fits the end of the lag screw. A six-point socket is usually favorable for this job.

As with spikes, the top log should be predrilled so that the lag screws can be screwed easily into the logs, resulting in less torque on the electric drill. The heads of the lag screws should be countersunk below the top of the log so that they will not hold up the log above. Be careful when using an electric drill or impact tool to install the lag screws. If you hit a knot or the heartwood, the drill can twist and cause injury to you. The power of these tools can work for you, but they can also work against you if you are not extremely careful.

Bright-steel lag screws or galvanized lag screws are available. Some come with the machining oil still on them, which can be helpful. If you have trouble getting the screws into the logs, lubricate the threads with a small amount of oil. Placing a washer in a one-and-a-half-inch hole countersunk about one-half inch into the log can also increase the holding power of the lag screws.

Besides being easier to install than spikes, which must be hammered into the logs, lag screws are easy to remove by reversing the electric drill and screwing them out. This may be a necessity if a log is placed in the wrong location or if it needs to be moved for any other reason, such as when you are placing the first logs (the sill logs). You may have to move the sill logs around a bit to get them square and in their proper location. With the lag screws, you merely remove the screws, move the log to the correct spot, and then screw the lags back in place. On the sill logs, don't sink the lag screws all the way down into the subfloor until you are certain that all the logs are where they belong for this first row; then, screw the lag screws tightly into the subfloor.

Log Screws

A fairly recent innovation in the log construction industry is the coated log screw. Coated log screws can be obtained in lengths from six inches to fourteen inches. They are smaller in diameter than lag screws, ranging from one-eighth inch to one-fourth inch in diameter depending on the manufacturer. They are coated to resist the extractives that may be contained in the logs.

They are gaining in popularity because they do not require predrilling. You merely use an adapter in your electric drill to put the log screws into the solid log. This speeds up the log-laying process and requires less work than driving in spikes or predrilling for lag screws.

Seek advice from an engineer about the correct spacing and the proper length of log screws to use on your log home. Building codes vary across the country.

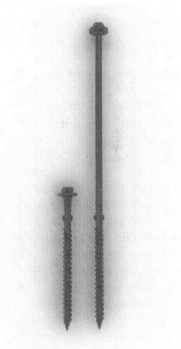

Thru-bolts

Some log-home manufacturers use thru-bolts, which are run completely through the vertical wall of logs. Thru-bolts facilitate settling in the log wall when shrinkage takes place in unseasoned logs. Thru-bolts can be hooked to one another with a collar. In this way, the builder does not need to use one eight- or ten-foot thru-bolt but attach a number of shorter bolts as the log wall is erected. Some manufacturers use

Log screws. Photo courtesy of the authors..

large springs on top of the last log, which is attached to the thru-bolts. The springs add pressure to the wall of logs, causing the logs to settle during the shrinking process. If they settle in an orderly progression, air leaks will not develop between successive courses of logs. As nearly every manufacturer has its own style, size, and method of using thru-bolt systems, follow its instructions exactly so you will not encounter problems later on. This advice pertains to all the components in the log-home package—from logs to caulk to gasket to lag screws. Don't read the instructions after everything else has failed.

Sealing the Logs

The final phase of building a log home is sealing the logs. Protecting your new home against weather, insects, and other damage will let you enjoy your home for many years. Following are some tips on sealant methods.

Gasket

Gasket material is a required component of a log home; it is the final seal to keep outside things out and inside things in. It functions like the gasket on the head of an engine or the weather stripping around a door. Even if your log wall is made with a tongue-and-groove system, the gasket is still required. If you buy a kit package, the manufacturer will include the gasket it recommends for the logs. For best results, follow the manufacturer's advice and use the gasket with the kit. Unless you are an experienced log builder, you probably don't know much about the different gaskets on the market and would likely buy an inferior product, causing leakage problems later.

Polyvinyl Chloride Gasket (PVC)

This closed-cell gasket is among the most popular gasket materials on the market. It is used not only in the log-home industry but also in the automotive, appliance, and commercial industries.

This gasket has a good "memory," so after heavy compression, it rebounds and fills the gap that results from shrinkage or other movement in the logs. Furthermore, it keeps water out of the house because it does not absorb any moisture that might reach it during a rainstorm.

The PVC gasket for log homes usually has an adhesive on one side, which is covered with a strip of paper for protection. Remove the paper prior to placing the gasket over the tongue(s) of the log. The adhesive will not stick if the logs have been subjected to rain or snow, so keep your logs covered and dry at all times, including at night. Cover the log walls at the end of each day to prevent them from getting wet during the night. This saves delays in construction the next day. Also, we do not advise using strips of gasket at butt-and-corner joints because they will hold the logs apart. At butt-and-corner joints, caulk plus a spline forms the best seal. Always remember that logs do not shrink lengthwise.

Impregnated Foam

Some products on the market are composed of open-cell foam that has been impregnated with a tar-like substance. This tar-like substance repels water and adds a sticky coating to the gasket, which seals any space that results from shrinkage, settling, or movement in the log. This foam is used in the same manner as the PVC gasket. Take care in storing this and any foam gasket material. If left in the sun, it could become a sticky mess. You should store all gaskets in a cool, dry place to prevent them from becoming degraded by heat or

Thru-bolt.
Drawing courtesy of the authors.

moisture. Always follow the manufacturer's specific recommendation for storing the material and for applying it to the logs.

Open-Cell Foams

These foams are not prevalent in the industry today. They are basically foam strips with air holes. This is a first-generation gasket material for several reasons.

First, the open-cell construction can absorb water (i.e., rain). When the gasket holds water, it decays over time. Second, it does not have a memory, so after being compressed for a period of time, it cannot expand with the changing conditions of the logs, allowing air and water to leak into the log home. A gasket is used to fill voids that result from shrinkage and settling of the logs or a low tongue on a log. Thus, this type of gasket by itself is not a good choice for a final gasket seal.

Caulk

Using a flexible caulk. Photo courtesy of Sashco.

The purpose of caulk (higher performing caulks are called sealants) is to seal joints or cracks from the intrusion of water, air (either hot or cold), dust, pollution, insects, and noise. Caulk can also serve the merely aesthetic purpose of dressing up or finishing off an otherwise rough joint. To better understand sealants, let's compare sealants and adhesives. Sealants are used to seal joints that move, and adhesives are used to prevent joints from moving. Some people use caulk to seal the spaces over the tongues of wall logs. The drawback is that if the logs shift to any degree, the caulk must have resiliency, or it will not move enough to seal any gap that may occur.

Caulk is best used at butt-and-corner joints of the logs as an added seal to the spline system. It can also be used around windows and doors to obtain a tight seal at the log window jamb area and between the jamb and the windows or doors. After your log home has been up for six months to a year, you can use a small amount of caulk at butt-and-corner joints or in any fairly large cracks in the natural logs around the home.

We advise you to use only the best-performing sealants for these purposes. Your circumstances may dictate the definition of "best." Generally, the best-performing sealants have great elasticity and adhesion. You may also consider the following attributes when determining the best sealant for a particular job:

- Speed of sealant cure
- Paintability
- Ease of application
- Ease of cleanup

- Odor and health effects of working with the sealant
- Cost (especially when the total project cost is considered)
- Shrinkage of the sealant
- Toughness (or abrasion resistance)
- Chemical resistance
- Heat or cold resistance
- Ability of the sealant to adhere to but not damage a surface

The chemistry of a sealant does not determine whether it is right for your job. Some "100 percent acrylic" caulks can perform much worse than other "100 percent acrylic" caulks. (The same can be said for siliconized acrylic latex caulks and other types of sealants.) Check with the manufacturer for actual performance information. Cured physical samples supplied by some manufacturers are also good indicators of performance, especially if you can compare them to other cured samples. Be sure to understand the difference between the terms elasticity and flexibility. Finally, caulk is not to be used as a substitute for good construction.

Chinking Compounds

Chinking. Photo courtesy of Sashco, Inc.

Chinking is an elastic, synthetic material that resembles mortar. Chinking allows movement of the logs and provides a maintenance-free weather seal. In existing log homes, chinking is used to fill cracks that have developed between the horizontal surfaces of the logs due to shrinkage, weathering, or just old age. In some cases, homeowners have chinked the exterior (and interior) of their homes to achieve an authentic look of days gone by. We see this quite often on round,

Swedish-coped logs, handcrafted log homes, and square logs with dovetail corners.

Chinking isn't what it used to be. No longer is mortar applied over chicken wire. Now, chinking is made from chemical compounds that create a
product that looks like caulk but is very resistant to the elements. When it dries, it is very tough and can withstand extremes of heat and cold and wet and dry. A number of colors are available to match the surface on which it is used.

Chinking can be applied either by filling small cracks with chinking only or by using backer rod, which we will discuss later in this chapter, in conjunction with the chinking for large cracks. When you use backer rod for large cracks, you need less chinking to fill the void, and a tight seal results. The backer rod has a certain resiliency, so it can move with the changing climate during the course of the year. For specifics on the various chinking/backer-rod combinations on the market, contact the manufacturers of these products. Suppliers of this material advertise in log-home magazines, which can be found at the larger bookstores.

Chinking comes in small or large tubes. For large jobs, you can purchase a five-gallon bucket. You can apply the chinking by using a large caulking gun, which is filled from the bucket, or by using a pump apparatus, which consists of a gun at the end of a long hose. A compressor supplies the pressure to push the chinking through the hose. For a complete log home, using the compressor-type unit is quicker and easier than using countless tubes of chinking and a caulking gun.

Before staining over the chinking, consult with the manufacturer. Some types of stains may not stick to the chinking or may discolor it. Apply chinking and caulk to a clean, dry surface. Always check with the manufacturer of all your log-home products for their specific application procedures, safety considerations, and their lifespans.

Backer Rod
Backer rod is a solid strip of extruded foam that is placed in log joints to provide a surface that chinking won't adhere to. When backer rod is installed behind chinking, it enables the chinking to stick only at the top and bottom of the joint where it makes contact with the log. When the logs shrink or expand, the material is pulled only in two directions. If backer rod is not used, the chinking will stick to all parts of the log and not be able to stretch properly when the logs move.

Backer rod has full-round, half-round, trapezoid, and triangular cross sections and can be composed of either open-cell or closed-cell foam. In open-cell foam, the cells or bubbles in the foam are broken, and air fills the spaces in the material. Open-cell backer rod is easy to install because it is soft and compresses to fit most joints. Open-cell backer rod is able to absorb moisture, which allows chinking and caulk to dry faster. While this may be a benefit, it can quickly become a drawback if it is used on the exterior of a home, as water may accumulate inside the open cells and create the conditions for rot to occur.

Closed-cell foams occur when the cells inside the foam remain intact. This type of backer rod is a good choice for exterior use because it does not hold moisture and repels water.

Butt-and-Corner Joints

Although logs do not shrink longitudinally, sealing the vertical joints on a log home is still important. This is done using splines and caulk. Putting the logs together tightly during the construction phase is also important. We will discuss this procedure in detail below.

Splines

The log-home industry supplies a number of different spline systems. They can be made of steel, plastic, or wood. Some builders have even used expanding foam in a void at butt-and-corner joints to make a tight seal. Let's consider the normal procedure for placing a log with a spline.

Before setting the next log in place, put a small bead of caulk on the end of the log that is already in place. A small amount is all you need, as you do not want to have caulk squeezed out past the log, creating an unsightly appearance. Gently push the log being installed up against the log that is already spiked down. Now, with a sledgehammer, tap the end of the log being installed so that is tight against the other log. When the log is properly aligned and pushed tightly against the guide braces, use a 20d nail or a six-inch or eight-inch log screw to hold it securely against the other log. Now, attach this log to the one below with spikes or screws, being careful not to dislodge the log from the guide braces.

Next, it is time to place the spline(s). Use an electric drill and proper bit to drill the required pilot hole where the two logs join. This hole may be one-half inch to one inch in diameter, as most splines are in this size range. By drilling a pilot hole, you make driving in the spline easier. The hole should be slightly larger than the spline so that the spline will not spread the logs apart when it is driven into the joint. We have seen some splines that were actually two-by-fours cut to the proper length. However, this is overkill because logs do not shrink lengthwise. If unseasoned logs are used in the construction of a log home, the corner joints are an area of concern. If the logs shrink, they can pull apart at the corners; thus, pay special attention to corners, more so than to regular butt joints.

Dowels

One of the most common methods of sealing butt-and-corner joints is to use a wood dowel cut to the suitable length. The diameter of these dowels ranges from five-eighths inch to one inch. It is a simple way to effectively seal joints, and the materials are readily available. For a five-eighths-inch dowel, drill a three-fourths-inch pilot hole. Again, do not drill the pilot hole too small, or the logs will be pushed apart when the dowel is driven into the pilot hole. Some builders place caulk in the pilot hole before driving in the dowel, but this is merely a personal preference. We feel that caulk is unwarranted, especially if the dowel fits snugly in the hole. Furthermore, if too much caulk is placed in the pilot hole, hydraulic pressure can push the logs apart when the dowel is driven into the pilot hole, creating quite a mess when the caulk squirts out around the joint.

Planning to Build

Chapter Highlights

- Before deciding to build a log home yourself, consider your skill level, time commitments, and access to helpers.

- A contractor-built home has numerous considerations for a consumer. Selecting a contractor and obtaining a clear contract, proper licensing, insurance, bonding, and correct permits are crucial.

- Home-site selection should account for the physical characteristics of the site itself, environmental factors, and legal issues.

Once you've decided that a log home is right for you, you must decide how and where you'll build your home. From doing it yourself to working with a contractor to site selection, educating yourself about the overall process is wise.

How Much Does a Log Home Cost to Build?

Most people ask about cost before posing any other questions they might have on log homes. Although their concern about money is understandable, the answer to their question isn't so simple. As for any home, the cost of a log home depends on many factors.

The most basic consideration is where you want to build the log home. Is it destined to be a mountain resort in California or Colorado or an elite retreat in New York state? Or do you plan to put it on a remote, rural property in Arkansas or North Dakota? Construction and materials costs vary dramatically from region to region, reflecting the cost of living, so you'll probably pay more to build a log home in California than in Arkansas. Some locations put greater legal demands on contractors or engineers, with state or local agencies requiring permits. Others have fewer or no building codes, and don't make engineers or contractors jump through quite so many hoops.

Location, of course, is just the beginning. Consider these other factors that directly affect the cost of a log home:

- **What type of log-home components do you want?** Do you want a precut package, a custom, handcrafted log home, or random-length logs from the local sawmill? The price of these components can vary greatly, as will the final cost of the home.

- **Will shipping be involved?** Do you intend to ship logs from another part of the country so that you can get precisely the home and home plan you desire? Shipping will very likely increase costs; but as a relatively small percentage of the total costs involved, it probably won't be prohibitively expensive.

- **What do you plan for the foundation or basement?** Do you want a full basement, maybe even completely finished? Or will you be content with a slab foundation or a crawl space? Each form of construction will have its own impact on costs.

- **What type of ceiling do you want?** Log walls make up just a small portion of the material costs. The type of ceiling affects the cost, too, whether made of exposed beams, conventional two-by-four rafters, or a truss. Cost also depends on your choice of regular asphalt shingles, shake shingles, or a metal roof.

- **What interior features do you need?** Most people have the misconception that once the house is shelled in, they are almost done. But interior options can quickly run up the costs of both materials and labor. Imagine the budget-destroying effects, for example, of hardwood floors, a custom stone fireplace, handcrafted cabinets, top-of-the-line bathroom and kitchen fixtures, specialty lighting and electrical components, and interior wall finishes.

Estimating costs

Once you have answers to such questions, you can begin to estimate the actual cost of the particular log home you are thinking of building. Use the following process to help you arrive at your estimate more easily and accurately:

- **Check local building costs.** Call local builders or contractors or other people who have built homes of any kind to find out some particulars on building costs in your area. If custom homes are being built in the area for $125 per square foot, for example, then use that figure as a guide. The square-foot building cost will give you a better idea of how big a home you can afford to build.

- **Find a log-home company and get blueprints.** Once you're sure you can afford that ballpark square-foot building cost, you can start shopping for the right company to provide the log package you need. A good log-home company should be able to provide detailed blueprints for the home you want, whether it's one of their predesigned packages or a home designed for your personal tastes and needs. You will need blueprints from the log-home company—or from an architect experienced in designing log homes—to bring to the contractor who will actually put up the building.

- **Bring in a builder.** Again, ask around for reputable builders in the area who have experience with log homes. It's fair to ask for references, to talk to past clients, and to see homes the builder has actually built. Once you find prospective builders, you will need to bring completed blueprints, along with specifics on the flooring, cabinets, roofing, and so on that you want. The builder will have to look at your lot to see if putting in a foundation, septic system, driveway, and other fundamentals will require more or less work than normal. And remember, that per-square-foot cost you researched for your area won't cover those deluxe bathrooms or kitchens, teak floors, imported crystal lighting fixtures, or other dream items. Keep your feet on the ground when planning your home—unless, of course, you are free of financial constraints.

- **Beware of simple multiplication formulas.** You might hear that a completed log home costs maybe two or three times the price of your log. But that kind of popular formula is not an accurate judge of the cost of a finished log home. One package, for example, may sell for $30,000 while another of comparable size is $60,000, but the less expensive package may include fewer finished materials. Applying the two- or three-times multiplier to the lower and higher prices would give you a range of $90,000 to $180,000 for a completed home, which isn't an accurate estimate. Remember, components that go into a log home, or any home, can vary greatly in price from the low end to the high end. Which end of the price spectrum you're aiming for will impact the final cost of the home. The final, only reliable way to estimate the finished cost of your log home is to ask one or more builders to review your blueprints after you have told them exactly what kinds of materials, finishes, and components you want in the house.

- **Buffer your budget.** It's always smart to include in your budget a buffer of 5 to 10 percent to cover price increases or unforeseen expenses. If you are on a really tight budget, don't just throw caution to the wind and say, "Let's just build it, and it will all work out." That definitely falls under the category of "famous last words." Yes, things might work out. But if you are wrong, you—or the bank—may end up owning a not-quite-completed log home.

I have worked with many people who start out wanting their dream home, a log home with the best of everything. Their dreams become reality when they discover that they cannot get a loan to cover such a project. Eventually, they go for a conventional, factory-built home because it is less expensive. But if they had instead done their research and planning first and started with a more realistic floor plan with fewer bells and whistles, they could have had a log home that would have fit their budget and come far closer to making their dreams come true.

Be realistic when setting goals for your new log home. Don't design something that is completely out of your financial range. The belief that log homes are very expensive to build is just not true. Too many people go about planning and budgeting for log homes in the wrong way and needlessly run up the price.

Doing It Yourself: Some Important Considerations

"Can we build it ourselves?" is the first thing that many people ask us. It is part of the pioneer spirit: people think they can build a log home with their untrained family members when they would never consider building a conventional home with them. In considering whether to take on building your log home as a do-it-yourself project, consider three major factors: your skill level, the amount of time you can commit to the project, and the amount of labor you can count on from friends and family. Doing it yourself certainly has advantages, but you must also think about the disadvantages.

Certainly, doing it yourself can simplify the process of building a log home. You will have no contracts to read and sign, and you will not have to adhere to a contractor's time schedule. You will not have to write checks for labor or deal with subcontractors, and you will have no one to blame for shoddy work except—you guessed it—yourself.

Doing the construction yourself will be less expensive overall—if you are successful. If you can do most or all of the construction and general contracting, you could save 25 percent or more on the cost of a new home. The home could be built in six to eight months at a substantial savings and out of quality materials with quality construction. If you make purchases carefully, you could also save money on raw materials including studs, plywood, trusses, Sheetrock, lights, and bathroom fixtures, while keeping your eyes open for sales or discounted models of sinks, bathtubs, and more.

You gain a feeling of personal accomplishment when you construct your home alone from start to finish, because this is a home that was built by you, the homeowner. However, if rain runs down the inside of the walls and wind blows through cracks in the joints, it will not be a home that you will want to brag about to your friends and family.

Skill Level

A finely finished home contains quality construction and materials throughout. Your log home must meet building codes during the first visit by the building inspector. When constructing your own home, you should follow the national building codes that are applicable for your state—even if there are no formal codes in your county. If you ever plan to sell your log home, it must also stand the test of intense scrutiny by a possible buyer.

Only you can decide the answer to the question "Can I (or my family) build it?" You must be very honest with yourself and your family. If you think that you can build your own home, and you really can't, then you are sure to try the stability of your marriage, financial resources, and mental health. When you finally throw down the hammer and saw and walk away from the job, you will have lost the backing and probably the respect of those who were counting on you. So, let's deal with some of the hard questions that you need to ask yourself:

- Have you ever worked in the construction trades before?

- If so, how long have you worked in the trades?

- Are you a skilled framer, or are you a "go-for" (as in, "go for this and go for that")?

- Can you or have you ever put down a subfloor?

- Can you cut rafters with a framing square?

- Can you install or have you ever installed roofing?

- What do you know about electricity and plumbing?

- Can you size the joists and rafters so that they will be structurally sound for local snow loads, wind loads, and dead loads?

- Can your friends or relatives help? Do they know anything about construction? Remember, many friends and relatives are "sunshine soldiers" who may not show up after the going gets rough or as the project continues month after month.

On all of the above points (and there are many more), you must be entirely honest with yourself. Once you make a commitment to build the house with "sweat equity," turning back can be hard. If you decide to hire help later, you may run into financial problems due to the increased cash outlays required by a legitimate contractor. Think about this seriously before attempting to build your own log home.

Time

Besides having the expertise to build your own log home, you must have plenty of time. Do not think that you can carry on the construction over a year's time by working only on weekends. If you work only on weekends, months will pass before the home is closed in tight from the weather. In the meantime, the logs and subfloor will be rained or snowed on. This will cause the delaminating of the plywood or wafer board. You will be unable to install the finished floor on the uneven surface. The logs will get wet and sun-bleached as they sit in the weather, waiting to be installed. You will also lose a lot of time setting up, getting the tools out at the beginning of the workday, and putting the tools away and covering everything when the day is over.

Helping Hands

Needless to say, you cannot build the home without some help. You need to have an extra person or two to help with the project. It will decrease the stress and save you on backaches. The extra help will also add to the safety of the job site. We are talking about adults who know how to work, not young people hired from the neighborhood. Magazines sometimes show the whole happy family in the process of building their log home, children and all. Keep children away from the job site, and hire competent help to aid you in the safe and efficient construction of your home.

Contractor-Built Home

If doing the job yourself isn't an option, then consider hiring a licensed contractor. This will result in less physical strain for your but will add labor costs. The cost of the contractor will include workers' compensation coverage, as well as insurance and other overhead, which would not be required if you built the home yourself. The contractor's profit is also part of the equation. Contractors do not work for wages; they want to make a profit.

Selecting a Contractor

Don't select a contractor based solely on price. That is a poor way of doing business. You should research the reputation and level of expertise of a number of contractors. After you have found several who have experience, who have an excellent reputation, and who have lived in your area for a number of years, you can move along in the selection process. Checking with the contractors' past clients and viewing their work are good next steps. You can also ask the local building suppliers about a contractor's reputation and skill. If subcontractors are eager to do work for them, the contractors are likely skilled, honest business people.

After you select a contractor, you can get prices for the work that you want done. Remember to provide the contractors with your detailed blueprints so that they can make accurate estimates. Get all estimates in writing, and stay away from "ballpark" bids; a bid that is not detailed and accurate isn't worth the time it takes to write. Ask your chosen contractors to bid the project using the same materials and labor. In this way, you can compare "apples with apples" and not have several dissimilar bids.

Furthermore, think of the contractors' time in doing bids. Sending a bid out to half the contractors in the yellow pages while knowing you will only choose one is not a good idea. Obtaining too many bids leads to confusion and wastes people's time. Reputable builders require several months notice before taking on another project, so give your chosen builder four or five months' lead time. But be mindful that if you get a bid several years in advance, the bid will have to be redone prior to contract signing.

When you are in the preliminary stages of planning, you can ask a local contractor to estimate the current per-square-foot cost of new homes in your area; this estimate is for planning purposes only and should not be misconstrued as a ballpark bid. If homes are being built for $125 to $150 per square foot, and you can only afford $90 to $100 per square foot, then you need to downsize. Don't design a champagne home if you have a beer budget. Do not waste everyone's time in bidding your home if you really can't afford it or if you are not serious. We often hear contractors complain about this.

Some contractors may charge a fee for preparing a turnkey estimate. The contractors may refund this fee when you hire them. This fee is reasonable, as estimating a home takes several days.

The Construction Contract

Around 1760 BC, the Babylonian king named Hammurabi wrote a code of laws. Within this text lie history's first laws protecting the consumer against shoddy construction. In 1904 Robert Francis Harper translated the codes in his book "The Code of Hammurabi, King of Babylon." The code states: "If a builder build[s] a house for a man and do[es] not make its construction firm, and the house which he has built collapse[s] and cause[s] the death of the owner of the house, that builder shall be put to death." Since then, construction laws have changed quite a bit but have not lost their seriousness.

A Good Contract

A good contract and a good set of blueprints will save countless headaches during construction. What is a good contract? One legal commentator characterizes a good construction contract in the following terms:

A good contract clearly informs each party what it must do and to what it is entitled. It also informs each party of its rights if the other party does not perform as promised. It anticipates the likely problems and resolves them clearly and in a way that strikes the parties as reflecting a proper allocation of risks and responsibilities [emphasis added]. A good construction contract, of course, includes well-drafted drawings and specifications that inform the contractor what it must do to earn the promised compensation and provides a method of determining whether the objective has been reached. A good construction contract also reflects the realities of contract administration and does not require procedures not likely to be followed. A good contract principally provides a set of working rules for the parties and secondarily addresses judges or arbitrators who may be called upon to interpret it. (Sweet, J. *Sweet on Construction Industry Contracts*, Hoboken, NJ: Wiley Law Publications, 1992, 21.)

Always ask an attorney to review the contract for any flaws or legal loopholes. A good contract protects you as well as the contractor. You can turn to it if something unforeseen comes up during the construction of the home. Don't try to write your own contract at your kitchen table. This will cause headaches down the road if questions arise.

Standard Forms

Standard forms should not be used without modifications. Because they are drafted for broad applicability, standard contracts cannot account for all transaction-specific and jurisdiction-specific terms that the parties need in their agreement. For example, a particular state's laws may require that indemnities be written in a certain way to be legally effective.

Do not become "contract complacent." Read the contract, even if it is a standard form. New projects or circumstances may necessitate a fresh look at specific boilerplate language.

Every contract contains the bias of the drafter. Bias is an inescapable element of any contract, whether drafted by the counsel for one of the contracting parties or by an industry organization. Knowing both the relative merits of and the circumstances under which to use the various standard forms published by different industry organizations is essential. Consult an attorney if the builder does not have a contract. If the builder does provide a contract, ask your own attorney to look for flaws that could result in future problems.

Licensed Contractors

Contractors hate to admit that getting into their field can be no tougher than printing up a business card. In some states, that's all a person needs to get into the act. Many states do require contractors to be licensed, but laws vary widely. Some states administer rigorous skills testing, while others merely collect a fee. Still, any license will afford some protection. Check with your state attorney general's office or with the Department of Consumer Affairs to see if your state issues licenses. If so, insist that your contractor have one, and note the number on your contract. Using an unlicensed contractor in an area that requires licensing might invalidate your contract.

Permits

Contractors are normally responsible for getting all necessary permits on a remodeling job, but some start work without them. Why? Depending on how efficient your local bureaucrats are, it can take months for the city or county to issue a basic permit. Getting plans approved by a co-op, condo board, or a city's landmarks commission can take even longer. Some homeowners choose to collude with their contractors to avoid expense and delays, but the owners are legally and financially responsible if the infraction is discovered. And run, don't walk, away from any contractor who asks you to get the permit. He may be trying to limit his responsibility.

Some localities won't issue permits until the job site has been inspected for environmental hazards such as lead, asbestos, or radon. Make sure your contractor knows how to check for these substances and is able to dispose of them properly or find someone who can.

Insurance and Bonding

Finally, make sure your contractor has at least two kinds of insurance: liability (for property damage) and workers' compensation (for his employees). Ask to see the original certificate, or call his agent. Make sure that your contractor is bonded. Bonds are risk-transfer instruments in which a third party, the surety, assumes the risk of the contractor's performance and the risk of the contractor's payment obligations to certain subcontractors and suppliers for a particular project in return for a premium payment. Owners (or their lenders) may require the transfer of these risks, which is accomplished by stipulating in the construction contract that the contractor furnish the owner with performance and payment bonds. The contractor then obtains bonds from a surety, who has assessed the contractor's capacity to perform and financial strength. The surety's issuance of the bonds serves as further assurance to the owner that the contractor is qualified for the project.

One Contractor, One Job

Some who have embarked on a remodeling odyssey have stories about how it cost twice as much and took twice as long as expected. Some delays—weather, termites, and acts of God—are unavoidable. But you shouldn't have to put up with a skeleton work crew or an irregular work schedule. Those are warning signs that your contractor is distracted by another job. Get a commitment from your contractor to work from about 7:30 a.m. to 4:30 p.m., five days a week. Ask to meet the foreman, and get an idea of how many workers will be on the site daily.

Another common schedule saver is to insert a lateness penalty clause in your contract as well as an incentive for early completion. Most experienced contractors consider a penalty clause standard.

Retention

Retention is the storage or holding back of something. In construction, you hold back money. The contractor should never have more of your money than he has spent. The most common payment schedule is one third up front, one third at some construction milestone midway through, and one third at the end. However, unless your contractor is ordering expensive, custom-built items such as kitchen cabinets, you should write a contract that keeps your first payment to 10 or 15 percent. Most contracts also include standard language that allows you to hold back part of each progress payment until the entire job is complete to your satisfaction. Paying everything up front can leave you at risk if the contractor drops your project and moves on to another one or to another state.

Lien Wavers

Always get lien waivers from the contractor and from all subcontractors when you pay them for work completed. This protects you from subcontractors or suppliers who have not been paid by the general contractor. Lien waivers state that you have paid everyone who was involved in the work performed. Thus, these same people cannot come back to you for payment if they have not been paid in full by the contractor or subcontractor.

Home Site Selection

Once you've decided who will build your log home, the location of your log home also impacts your decision to do it yourself. Here are a few items to keep in mind selecting a site.

Physical Characteristics

There are many things to look at beyond aesthetics when choosing a home site. The first things to note are the site's physical dimensions, layout, and topographical features. Is the site near a lake, a river, or the ocean? Is any portion unsuitable for building, such as a pond? Check the grade, or slope, as well as the compass orientation. Study the soil composition: does it consist of sand, Clay, or rock? These factors will affect the excavation, bearing capacity, and foundation. Also, find out if any of the property is on a landfill or hazardous waste site.

Environmental Factors

Environmental factors are often overlooked part during home site selection. A log home should be protected as much as possible from the elements. If you have trees on your property, the home can be sited so that the trees will protect the home from wind, rain, and snow. This must be done with caution, as you do not want to build the home next to large trees in their final years of life. You also do not want to build the home so close to the trees that excavation will cut their roots and result in their deaths within a few years.

It is worth mentioning that you should also know what is under the soil surface. Are you on a rock outcropping that will require blasting to get a foundation installed? Will you have problems with the septic tank or leach field due to soils that do not allow fluids to move though them? Your site should be slightly raised, not in a hole, which would result in water problems. Consider the aspect of your home; do you want the morning sun to come through the kitchen window, for instance?

Think about your geographic region and the elements' impact on your home. If you're building in the north, consider facing the solid wall of the garage to the north to catch the winter winds. In the south, you may want the main living space to face north so that the sun's heat won't overheat the areas where you spend most of your time. Think of the wind, rain, snow, and sun when you position your home.

Need some help? Check with architectural or energy firms listed in the local telephone book. Some firms may have computer programs that can determine that most energy-efficient orientation for your home. They can even locate windows in your home to maximize the amount of light and minimize cost and energy consumption. A service fee is normally charged on a square-foot basis.

Legal Issues

Home site selection must also be based on legal issues. With the help of your architect, research zoning laws concerning building height, size, materials, and distance from property lines. If you're building in a historic area, regulations regarding the exterior of the house might be quite extensive. In some parts of the country, water and mineral rights should also be investigated.

Building to Last

Chapter Highlights

- Plan ahead for the delivery of your log-home components, and prepare the job site for proper and safe storage of materials.

- Proper grading of your site will affect your foundation—a crucial element to your log home's stability.

- Proper construction techniques will save you time and money and prevent the need for excessive maintenance. Drip edges and roofs are especially crucial.

- Construction techniques to promote energy efficiency in your home are also important.

By this time, you should have a basic understanding of trees, logging, types of log-home packages, and log styles. Now, it is time to learn about building your log home.

As the saying goes, "An ounce of prevention is worth a pound of cure." This is certainly true of a log home. If it is worth building, it is worth taking care of. The owner of a log home may spend hundreds of hours a year taking care of the lawn, the trees, and the garden but may spend very little time taking care of the home itself. The first step in protecting your log-home investment is to build the log home a way that prevents undue assault by sun, rain, snow, and insects. During construction, you must be tuned into the many factors that will minimize the effects of the forces that can degrade your log structure. There are five steps to building a lasting log home:

1) Use proper construction techniques to keep the building site and the home dry.

2) Use a water-repellent exterior finish on the outside of the home.

3) Use a water-soluble wood preservative on the logs if you live in a humid area.

4) Maintain your log home by deflecting rain and keeping the home as dry as possible.

5) Make your home weather-tight, with no gaps and no air leaks.

Pre-Construction Concerns

Transportation and Delivery

After you purchase a log-home kit, it must be shipped to the building site. The same procedure is the same whether it gets shipped ten miles or a thousand miles. Before purchasing a log package, you need to know how the home will be shipped, how much you will be charged, and who will do the unloading.

Most log packages are sold "FOB," or "free-on-board," from the manufacturing plant. That means that the package will be loaded onto its trucks, a contract trucker, or your truck for free. After loading, the customer will be charged for the transport of the kit to the job site. It is safe to say that most log-home manufacturers do not have their own trucks, so they call contract truckers to come to the manufacturing plant and transport your materials,

The first question to ask is, "How much does delivery of my log home to the job site cost?" The manufacturer may give you a flat rate per load; put this in the contract. For example, the contract may specify two loads at $1,250.00 per load, and you know exactly what the freight will cost. If the rate is something like $1.50 per mile, then you will not know the freight charge until the truck arrives at your job site. In that case, the trucker hopefully won't have to take too many detours.

If the shipping is free, then check that log package is in line with other similar products. The manufacturer of the log kit may be including the shipping in the package price. If this is the case, then it is not free. With the price of transportation and raw materials going up, free shipping is less likely. However, this could be a way for a manufacturer to outdo the competition or offer a bargain, depending on how far the home has to be shipped.

If the price for transportation seems too high, call an over-the-road carrier listed in the telephone book to check the rates. Do not confuse an over-the-road carrier with a common carrier that just hauls smaller loads of materials across the state or country.

For short hauls, some log-home companies provide their own trucks with an unloading crane or forklift. This is not a common practice, so you should be prepared to obtain a forklift to unload your log materials at the building site.

The forklift should not be a small farm tractor with forks. It needs to be an off-road forklift with large tires to navigate the rough terrain at the job site. The small forklifts with small tires that one sees on loading docks are not suitable for this type of unloading. A minimum lifting capacity of five thousand pounds is the norm. Find out the weight of the bundles of building materials from the manufacturer. If you have trouble getting a forklift with a large lifting capacity, see if the log manufacturer can make the individual bundles smaller.

Unloading and placing the logs at the job site of some homes will require a crane. This is true if your handcrafted home uses large logs. The manufacturer may even provide the workers to set the logs properly.

Although we have seen small cranes and backhoes used for unloading, we do not recommend them. The straps used to lift the logs from the truck can slip, and the logs and other building materials can end up being dumped over the building site. It is a bad sign when the unloading goes wrong and your materials are already damaged before the building process has even begun.

For windows and doors that are delivered to the job site, have several helpers to get these off the truck and into the basement or storage shed. It is not the truck driver's responsibility to go up onto the truck and help unload. Some drivers may do this, but it is not part of their job. A note of caution: do not get on top of the load of logs and lumber during unloading. This is very dangerous.

If you absolutely cannot find a forklift to do the unloading, ask the manufacturer if unloading the logs by hand is possible. This is the last resort and is not recommended. If you have a number of helpers, it can be done, but the task will take some time. The clock is ticking, and the trucker will want to get paid for his downtime on the job site. Find out how much the driver will charge per hour of waiting before you attempt to unload by hand. We have to warn you about the possibility of injury when you do the unloading without the convenience of machinery.

An alternative to unloading on the job site is to unload at the local lumberyard where you are buying the rest of your building materials. Later, the logs can be hauled to the job site and unloaded by hand.

This is not the best-case scenario, so arrange well ahead of time to rent a forklift.

The first places to contact about forklifts are rental centers. Other places may have a forklift that they are willing to loan or rent, especially on weekends. Your contractor may be able to give you a hand with this search. However, don't let this particular responsibility languish until the day before the logs arrive, because then you will be in a panic to find a forklift. Unloading is the homeowner's responsibility; do it with a forklift and not with a bunch of impressed laborers that you consider friends. Friendships can be lost when too much is asked or if someone gets injured.

When your logs are shipped by the manufacturer of the kit, you want to know if the load is "tarped," or covered, to prevent damage to the logs and other materials. If the shipping distance is short, this may not be a problem. However, it is a big problem if the load goes through rain, snow, or a freshly tarred road. For long hauls, the load needs to be covered.

To protect your logs and building materials, the individual bundles should be wrapped in plastic. This can be plastic sheathing covering the complete bundle or shrink wrap protecting the materials from a dirty tarp used by the trucking company. Plastic will also protect the logs as they await assembly at the job site. If you are unloading in the rain, you will appreciate knowing that the logs will not get soaked and muddy. Likewise, it is wise to have all of the hardware and gaskets placed on a pallet and wrapped to prevent damage from rain, mud, or mishandling.

Normally, the windows arrive in cardboard boxes or wrapped in plastic to prevent damage. This is especially important with metal-clad windows. If they get dented or heavily scratched, they can be hard to repair and expensive to replace.

If the materials arrive damaged, who is responsible? If they are placed on the truck in a damaged condition, the trucker should note it and tell the company. If the trucker damages them due to poor strapping of the load or failure to tarp when he was paid for these services, then he would be responsible. If you or one of your employees drops a window during unloading, then you are responsible. At the time of unloading, note all damaged or missing materials on the trucker's shipping invoice as well as on the manufacturer's invoice. Don't call your supplier months later to report a damaged item.

The trucker is in charge of his or her truck. Don't ask the trucker to drive into a muddy field dotted with stumps or onto a steep grade.

If the trucker doesn't want to take the vehicle into some inaccessible building site, then his or her word is final. Don't try to be a hero by telling the trucker to let you drive the vehicle to the building site. You will only make yourself less popular with the driver, and that is not the way to start out the day.

If the building site is difficult for a forty-eight-foot tractor-trailer to get to and turn around in, then consider an alternate unloading site. This could be at an adjacent farm, with the owner's permission, or it could be in town at the lumberyard where you are buying your building materials, as mentioned earlier.

Take all of this shipment and unloading information seriously. Shipping and unloading are two of the simplest operations in the whole construction sequence, but they can become difficult quickly. Use a little common sense, and ask for the driver's opinion on the unloading operation. Drivers are there to help you, and they have experience in getting trucks to the final destination and unloading. Don't alienate them right from the beginning by telling them what they will do. Plan this out well in advance, and you won't have a problem.

We recommend that you put in a decent road to the building site with rock and gravel before construction begins. Don't wait until every truck that comes to the job site has gotten stuck and torn up the area. Once the driveway or building site gets torn up with ruts, things go from bad to worse, especially after it rains. In the end, you will have lots of towing bills, and the driveway will still have to be installed.

In a nutshell, planning, common sense, and courtesy will win the day as you unload your log home and other building components. It isn't hard unless you work to make it hard.

Grading, Clearing, and Grubbing

The first step that needs to be taken during construction is the grading of the lot. This is done before the foundation is started. Look at the lot and determine which way you will want the water from rain and melting snow to be diverted. You should then have the lot graded so that the water runs away from, not toward, the home. Needless to say, don't just direct it at your neighbor's yard or home. Deliberate thoughtfully here, and don't be afraid to talk with your builder or architect. After you make a decision, grade the lot and put in the appropriate drains and ditches so that problems with water in the basement and next to the foundation wall can be avoided.

If you are building in a wooded setting, examine the trees and shrubs that will be close to your future home. Take out any old or diseased trees. They are easy to overlook at this point, but they can cause a great deal of damage if they fall during a storm. Trees and shrubs too close to the home can also deflect rain toward the walls of your home—so they are a bad idea. We have seen people build their decks around a particular tree next to their homes. It may seem like a cute idea, but if this tree ever falls or if limbs are ripped from it in a storm, the homeowner will pay dearly for this oversight. A tree may look perfectly healthy, but its interior may be hollow, its demise awaiting a strong wind.

Construction Concerns

The Foundation

When the foundation is poured, be absolutely sure that a minimum of twelve inches of foundation are above the surrounding soil surface. This will help deter future damage by termites as well as from rain splash from heavy downpours. In high rainfall areas in the Pacific Northwest or the southeast, a minimum of eighteen inches is recommended. Before the foundation is backfilled, be sure to install foundation or French drains. French drains are ditches filled with gravel, rock that redirects ground and surface water away from an area. They are commonly used to prevent ground and surface water from penetrating or damaging building foundations. Lay them in the gravel and hook them to a storm drain or direct them toward a low area well away from the home. We have seen French drains that don't drain the water away from the foundation, as there is no outlet. The footings begin to sink as the water builds up around them, and the house as well.

Some people think a backfilled foundation makes for a convenient, sanitary landfill. Bottles, cans, waste wood, roofers felt, and more get thrown into the void around the foundation. The bottles and cans we can live with, but the excess wood buried around the perimeter of the foundation will only make the site more hospitable for wood-eating insects in the future. Wood buried around the building site and in the crawlspace will not attract insects per se, but after the insects land in the area, the wood provides the food and shelter to keep them there. You might say this in another way: if you don't want cockroaches in your home, don't leave food and garbage lying around unattended—this is the same principle.

In areas of high moisture and humidity, not only is a pressure-treated sill plate recommended for your foundation but also a pressure-treated box sill (rim joists) around the perimeter of the subfloor. This would not include the joists or the plywood subfloor but merely the exterior double-rim joists. Periodic wetting can occur in this lower, exterior area of the home. If the sill plate and double exterior header rots become infested with wood-boring insects, your house will be in structural limbo. Thus, in areas such as the southeastern or northwestern United States, you should install a pressure-treated box sill. Some may say that this is overkill; but when you're building a home, the small upfront cost is well worth the peace of mind. If you use a crawlspace in lieu of a full basement, be sure to put vents in the wall for ventilation. Also, put a vapor barrier over the soil surface in the crawlspace. This vapor barrier will prevent condensation on the first-floor joists and keep the moisture in the soil, not on the wood-supporting members.

Before we go onto other subjects concerning the log home, let's spend a moment on slab construction where a basement or crawlspace is not desired. In parts of the southern United States, slab construction is the norm, and basements and crawlspaces are not used due to water problems. In other parts of the country, problems with bedrock may make the slab a more practical alternative. Pouring a slab on the graded soil surface and leaving only a few inches between the soil surface and the logs is asking for trouble. A knee wall should be poured around the exterior of the slab to raise the logs above the surface of the soil. Fill can then be compacted within this knee-wall area.

The slab is poured over the fill and the required interior footings to prevent settling and shifting of the slab. There should be a vapor barrier between the slab and the soil surface and, in some areas, rigid insulation as well. This keeps moisture and cold from penetrating the slab and the home. This knee wall should be at least one foot above the soil surface. Homes can deteriorate if they sit mere inches above the soil surface. Rain splash and blowing rain can be enemies to the logs, and you won't need fifty years to find this out. In this age of synthetics and new materials, we too often forget about building practices from many years ago. If you start taking shortcuts in construction, you will see the effects later.

Log Construction

The log-construction phase varies with the log types and styles you are using. The following construction steps can be followed with the more widely used milled logs of uniform size. If you use logs cut from the forest or handcrafted logs, then the process will vary to some degree.

If you install the subfloor correctly to match the dimensions on the blueprints, the log installation process will be much easier and the results better. Some manufacturers require that you secure the logs with anchor bolts to a decay-resistant plate. If this is the case, then the logs must be drilled so that they can be placed down over the foundation bolts. Be careful to ensure that the logs are positioned properly so that the first-floor framing, loft joists, and rafters will fit properly later. Always check your dimensions; do not position the logs too far out or in. If this happens, other components will not fit properly later, and you can be out of square or plumb as the construction proceeds.

Your log-home supplier may require that the logs be installed on the subfloor. If so, build the subfloor according to the specifications on the blueprints. Be sure to use the correct rim-joist size so you can securely attach the logs to the subfloor superstructure.

After you install and secure the plywood, snap a line around the perimeter of the subfloor; this could be four, six, eight, or ten inches wide, depending on the size of the log. Your log supplier will provide this information. Let's say that you are using an eight-by-eight log, and a six-inch bearing surface is required. Snap this line six inches from the outside of the subfloor all around its perimeter. The interior surface of the log will be located on this snapped line. You must make allowances if your subfloor is out of square or is not quite built to the correct specifications. This is particularly important if the kit is precut. Measure from corner to corner to make sure that the snapped lines are square before proceeding. Do it slowly and accurately at this stage, and you'll save a lot of time later in the construction process.

If your logs are uniform in size, then you can place guide braces on this snapped line so that the logs will go up plumb and straight. If the logs are rustic and vary in diameter, you can use a chalk line as a guide. This chalk line will go down the center of the log wall and result in a wall that goes up plumb and does not bow out or in. Of course, you will have to move the chalk line up with each successive course of logs. Nail the guide braces to the subfloor with a rigid, diagonal brace back to the subfloor. If these braces are knocked out of plumb, then you will be following them with less-than-desirable results. Guide braces are usually constructed of 2×4s or 2×6s, which you can later recycle into the interior stud walls. If you are building with slab construction, then the interior walls can be installed and used as guide braces. To get a tight and straight corner, you should place good-quality 4×4s or 6×6s in it. This must also be braced with a diagonal 2×4 or 2×6 back to the subfloor. This corner brace can result in a very tight and aesthetically pleasing wall. Too often, corners are constructed poorly, resulting in air leaks.

Place the sill seal, gasket, and/or caulk on the subfloor prior to placing the first course of logs, called the sill logs or starter logs. It is advisable to start placing the logs at a corner of the log home. Secure the logs to the subfloor with the provided fasteners: spikes, lag screws, special log screws, or thru-bolts. Do not completely secure these fasteners until you place all of the logs on this first course and check for accuracy. If the logs are not correctly placed, you can withdraw the fasteners and move the logs. However, if the logs are fully secured to the subfloor withdrawing the lag screw or spike and moving the log to its correct location can be difficult. If you are satisfied with the location of the logs, screw the fasteners tightly to secure the logs in place.

If the logs arrive precut and numbered, then you must sort them. Place logs of the same type or in the same pile. You must keep these piles off the ground to prevent harm from dirt and moisture; lay two-by-fours or four-by-fours on the ground first. If you are using random-length logs, then you do not need to sort the logs, but you must take time to pick the right logs for the right position in the home. Don't cut sixteen-foot logs into short logs; they may be needed later as headers over the windows and doors.

Drill the pilot holes for the splines, and place the gasket and caulk as required. After checking that you have followed all of the manufacturer's steps, you can begin laying the next course of logs.

You should work from one corner of the log home at a time. You do not want to drag tools and extension cords all over the subfloor. Start at a door opening and lay logs around to another door or window opening. If you place logs around the home one course at a time, you will lose time moving tools and hardware about the subfloor.

To improve efficiency, give job descriptions to the various members of the crew. For instance, designate two people to bring up the correct logs as needed and to place them near their final point of installation. Designate two more people to lay the logs, and assign someone to caulk, lay gasket, and drill for any required splines.

For tight butt-and-corner joints, you should use log screws or 16d or 20d nails to pull the joints together before securing the logs.

Take your time during all phases of construction. Make sure that all steps have been completed before installing another course of logs.

The construction steps covered in this book are general guidelines to inform the novice builder of the many items that must be addressed during the construction phase. Specific procedures for your home will depend on the manufacturer and on your logs. This book will help you decide if you are qualified to tackle the job on your own. Be honest with yourself on this matter, because once you have set the building process in motion, there is no turning back.

Drip Edges

Some manufacturers mill a drip edge into the lower, exterior edge of the wall log. This is an added bonus, but it should not give the homeowner a false sense of security. This drip edge does not allow you to skip proper overhangs on the roof or provide all of the protection needed to keep your home maintenance free. It is just an added feature that will allow the logs to get wet during a violent thunderstorm backed by high winds. Rain will drip from the logs and not be pulled in between the logs by wind velocity or capillary action. For the drip edge to work as designed, the logs must be maintained with a water-repellent wood treatment. The rain must run off the logs and not soak into the wood.

Flashing

To keep wind and water from entering your home during violent weather, the tops of the windows and doors must be flashed with metal. Cut an upward-sloping saw kerf into the log above the windows and doors. Then, slip a piece of flashing into this slot and bend it down over the top of the window or door trim. Nail this in place with galvanized finishing nails. Don't go overboard, as only an inch or two of flashing bent down over the top trim is required. Some builders rely on the caulking gun for this job, but that provides only a short-term solution. Once the caulk shrinks or cracks, water will seep in during a rainstorm. Flashing is a preferred method for sealing windows and doors because you can paint the metal to match the logs.

Do not minimize this operation, as water can get through a crack that you cannot see with the naked eye.

If you have built a home with solid logs, but the gable ends are built up with a stud wall with exterior log siding, then flashing is also in order. Before putting on the first layer of log siding on the gable end, place a three- to four-inch piece of flashing over the studs, leaving one inch or two hanging over the top of the log directly below the siding. After you nail this flashing in place, you are ready to place the siding on the studs that make up the gable ends.

Porch Construction

We recommend that you build a porch instead of an uncovered deck because it will give you more protection from the elements. It will protect you from both the sun and the rain during weekend barbecues or while you are just relaxing. A porch roof will also deflect snow from the deck—in extreme cases, the snow's weight could tear an uncovered deck from the house.

A few items on porch and deck construction are critical for a well-built home. You must first tie the porch/deck superstructure to the piers and footings with specially designed hangers or metal straps. A gust of wind that might come up under the porch deck or porch roof would have to pull the footings and piers out of the ground to cause a complete failure. To merely "toe nail" the porch posts and other members together is structurally unsound. The porch stringers are attached to the porch posts with beam caps. The porch posts are, in turn, bolted to the concrete piers with steel straps called hold-downs embedded into the concrete. The piers are attached to the footings with steel as well. The porch deck and porch roof are held in place from below the soil surface.

The rafters should be connected to the main house and to the porch stringers using hurricane straps with plated deck screws.

All decking material and floor joists should be pressure-treated lumber. We recommend pressure-treated materials that are certified for below-ground as opposed to above-ground use. Buy the best so that you won't have a maintenance problem. The extra cost is worth it. High-grade redwood lumber is fine, but for joists it may not have the strength of pressure-treated yellow pine or hem fir. Plated deck screws are recommended over galvanized nails. They will not leave stains like unplated nails, and they will hold the deck in place during the periodic wetting and drying cycles. Remember that an open deck, which is exposed year-round to the weather, will require much more maintenance than a covered porch.

Second-Floor Loft

With the logs erected and the stud walls in place, you can put in the second-floor joists if your home will have a second floor or loft. In single-story homes, ceiling joists are sometimes used to give the effect of exposed beam rafters in the ceiling. These ceiling joists are generally smaller than the second-floor joists, as they do not have to support any significant loads in the attic.

The second-floor joists could be composed of conventional two-by-tens or two-by-twelves if the homeowner does not want beam joists. The floor can be soundproofed better with conventional dimension materials than with large-beam construction. (Without soundproofing, children running over the wood on the second floor will sound like a herd of elephants to those sitting downstairs.) The conventional joists would be finished on the bottom with Sheetrock or tongue-and-groove lumber. Sound-deadening insulation could be placed between these joists. The plywood, underlayment, and carpet are placed on the joists for a finished loft or second floor. This conventional second floor would be much quieter if you install carpet, though it is not an attractive alternative to many homeowners who want the rustic look of beams and tongue-and-groove flooring. This is a decision that you must make while designing the blueprints and before ordering materials for the log home.

Beam joists could be either standard-sized timbers, such as six-by-eights or four-by-tens, or they could be round logs, either turned or hand-peeled. Remember that strength of any given beam results from the depth of the wood; thus a four-by-ten can actually have more strength than a six-by-eight. Round beams may be large and heavy, but they may not carry the load of the second floor. Consult an engineer before you use these beams for the second floor. The second floor will not fall, but the floor can have spring in it when people walk or jump on it.

Gable Ends

The gable ends of the home, as well as the dormers, can be full logs, log cabin siding, or board and batten. The logs or log siding will fit the total look of the home much better than board and batten, but that is a personal preference.

If full logs are used for the gable, they should be stacked after the rafters are in place. In this way, you will have a guide to place the gable ends. This would be the case if the pitch cuts are made on the logs after stacking. If the gable ends are precut, check with the supplier for its recommendations. The log cabin siding and the board and batten would be placed over a conventional stud wall insulated like a conventional wall—with plywood and felt paper over the studs and under the siding. A vapor barrier would be placed on the inner, warm side of the wall. This could be covered with whatever is supplied with the kit or with Sheetrock, T&G paneling, or log siding.

Flashing should be installed over the last log of the log wall and under the log cabin siding or board and batten. This will prevent a blowing rain from seeping in under the log siding on the gable ends. Do not skip this operation.

Electrical

Some of the electrical components will be installed in the log walls. After you install the first or second course of logs, you should locate the electrical outlets in these logs. Local codes vary as to how high off the floor these electrical outlets must be located. A hole of one-and-a-half inches is drilled through the logs so that the electrical wires can be brought up from the basement or crawlspace. Using a plunge router, you can cut the logs to accept the outlet boxes. Be sure to space the outlets to meet codes. These codes ensure that any individual outlet will not be overloaded with appliances or lighting fixtures.

In most cases, the interior of the home will have stud walls. These walls facilitate the location of electrical wires, outlets, and switches. You can locate the switches next to doors by drilling the logs as they are stacked. This can also be done with exterior lights next to the exterior doors. Just drill the logs as you go up and then bring the wires to the exterior of the log by drilling the log to the outside of the home.

Electrical outlet detail. Drawing courtesy of the authors.

Another way to bring wires up next to the door for switches and lights is to rout the ends of the logs next to the door opening. Later, you will place the door jamb over the wires. This can be much simpler than drilling the logs as they are stacked.

You can take electrical wires to the second floor by going through the first floor stud walls to a stud wall located directly above on the second floor. You can also run wires between the bird block and through holes drilled in the rafters.

For hanging lights in a cathedral ceiling, the top of the rafters can be routed to accommodate the electrical wiring. This must be done prior to placing the decking over the rafters. Take care when nailing the decking down so as not to hit the electrical wiring. This would be the same method used for second-floor beam joists if lights will be hung from them.

Running wires through the logs by running a channel down the logs is not recommended. If a problem develops, it will be very hard to pull this wiring and then put it back in. Locate wiring to make it easy to install and easy to remove or repair if need be.

In slab construction, the logs would sit on a treated or rot-resistant sill plate. The wiring would be run along the sill plate and below the log, which will overhang the sill plate somewhat. This would later be covered with base trim. The interior stud walls can also be used to place electrical wiring, outlets, and switches.

For electrical work, we recommended that you use a licensed electrical contractor. If it is improperly done, the building inspector may make the unskilled electrician tear it all out and start over. A poorly installed electrical system could cause a fire, with dire results.

Plumbing

Those interested in a log home ask many questions about the installation of the plumbing. First of all, you do not put plumbing into the exterior log walls. Pipes would likely freeze in the winter, and they would be difficult to install.

The plumbing is placed in a "wet wall" in the interior of the home. This wet wall consists of two-by-six studs rather than the smaller two-by-fours. This allows you to install the various connections with adequate room. Thus, plumbing is installed in a log home the same way as in a conventional home.

It is a good idea to have as much plumbing as possible be "back to back." This means that the sink, commode, and tub would be aligned along one common wall to cut costs in the placement of the plumbing. The plumbing in the utility room could be located on a wall that has a bathroom on the other side. This cuts down on installation costs. Likewise, the bathroom on the second floor should be located over the bathroom on the first floor. This saves time and expense in installing the water pipes, drains, and so on. All of this should be shown on the blueprints prior to construction. The architect or contractor can help you in this planning process.

Scissor truss roof detail. Drawing courtesy of the authors.

The Roof

The roof is very important in protecting your log home. It is pertinent to look at some of the roof systems that are available for log homes. If you have not yet purchased a log-home package or selected the type of roof that you want to put on your log home, then this section will be of interest to you.

Truss Type

Truss-framed roofs are built from triangular-shaped, premade truss units. Trusses are premanufactured in a truss plant and are usually the least expensive option to support the roof. They are generally made of two-by-fours or two-by-sixes and are placed on the roof by a crane or a crew of men. Trusses are a common roof system in use today and have some big advantages:

- Trusses are incredibly strong.
- Because they are built strictly from shorter lengths of common-sized lumber (such as from two-by-fours), they are usually less expensive than other roof systems.
- Almost any shape of roof can be made with trusses.
- Because trusses prefabricated, they can be installed quickly.

Rafter Type

The rafter system takes more time to install and is more expensive than a truss roof. The rafters would not be exposed in the home, and they would consist of two-by-tens or two-by-twelves or floor truss material. These are the same materials that we discussed for the subfloor and look like an I beam made of two-by-fours and plywood.

In the most expensive roof system, the rafters are made of large beams. These could be four-by-eight or six-by-ten square beams or the more expensive, round, hand-peeled logs. Hand-peeled logs are more expensive due to the labor involved in making them and using them in construction. On both of these rafter types, two-by-six or two-by-eight tongue and groove is used as the decking over the exposed beam rafters.

You can also use a purlin system. These beam or log purlins run the length of the home and protrude at the gable ends to carry the roof overhang. The tongue-and-groove decking would be placed on top of the purlins.

Roof detail with trusses. Drawing courtesy of the authors.

A properly designed roof becomes a "cap" to protect the exterior of the home. People purchase windows that have an exterior cladding on them (aluminum or vinyl) so that they will have a maintenance-free home, but then they fail to design an adequate roof, and problems soon develop. Every time it rains, water runs down the windows due to inadequate overhangs. This can eventually result in leaks around the windows or water condensation between the double-glass panes. If clad windows are not used, then rotting can result on the window sill and/or frames.

Rafter system whith use of a mid-span purlin.
Drawing courtesy of the authors.

We recommend a five-foot overhang on the gable ends to protect the gable and the log walls below. This can be increased on particular designs that lend themselves to a large overhang, particularly on homes that have two stories of logs or have a large prow point filled with windows. The rafter tails should also have a large overhang to protect the side walls. This would normally be a two-foot overhang, but it will vary with the design of the home. On a ranch home with a 4/12 pitch, a two-foot overhang would be appropriate; but on a home with a 6/12 pitch, the rafter tails would hang too low and interfere with an out-swinging door or a screen door—tall people could hit their heads on the rafter tails. In many cases, the roof (including overhangs) will be twice the living area of the home.

The porch roof should carry the same five-foot overhang as the main roof. You should also allow for the maximum amount of rafter overhang on the porch. This will keep rain and snow from spilling onto it. A wraparound porch is pleasant to the eye and protects the home from the elements. This is a great idea in areas of high rainfall like the southeastern United States or the Pacific Northwest. The homeowners will have complete access around the home without ever having to go into the sun, rain, or snow. In hot areas, a porch will also shade the windows and cut air-conditioning costs. In northern climates, an enclosed porch will cut heating bills in the winter.

If a shed dormer is utilized on any portion of the home, it should have faux rafters between the shed dormer and the log wall below. Thus, the rafters' overhang on the dormer will protect the dormer, and the faux rafters will protect the logs below. If rain runs down the walls of your home, then you have done a poor job in designing your roof system. Follow these guidelines, and you will be ahead of the pack in protecting your log home.

This is an interesting point on roofs: In the United States, we build roofs with steep pitches and metal roofing so that the snow will slide off the roof and decrease the snow load. But in Switzerland, people build roofs with low pitches so that the accumulated snow will keep the home warm. Be careful when designing open decks under the roof area in high-snow-load areas. When the snow slides off the steep roof, it can tear the deck from the house and cause extensive damage.

Insulating the Roof

Do not skimp on insulation in the roof or ceiling area, as heat goes up and can easily be lost. When you use beam rafters or purlins in a roof, then you must install the insulation over the roof decking. This insulation can be either polystyrene or polyisocyanurate ridged-foam insulation. The polystyrene has about half the R-value of the polyisocyanurate. Here again, check with the building commission. In some areas, it may have codes against using certain types of rigid insulation due to toxic fumes that could be released in a fire.

Some manufacturers use rigid insulation that has plywood glued to the top of it; you install this over the roof decking by using pole barn nails or special screws supplied with the package.

Always remember to apply a vapor barrier on the warm side of the roof, as well as on the gable ends if conventionally framed. This will prevent condensation in these areas that could result in damage to the structure.

Example of a rafter roof system. Drawing courtesy of the authors.

One method of installing the sheets of rigid insulation that are not glued to plywood is to use "sleepers" on top of the roof decking. Place these sleepers sixteen inches on center from the eves of the roof up to the ridge, and cut the rigid insulation to fit between these sleepers

An air space is left between the plywood, which is nailed on top of the sleepers and rigid insulation. You must vent the roof system to prevent condensation. This results in a level roof on which to nail the shingles. Place roofer's felt over the plywood prior to placing the finished roofing materials: metal, cedar shakes, or asphalt shingles.

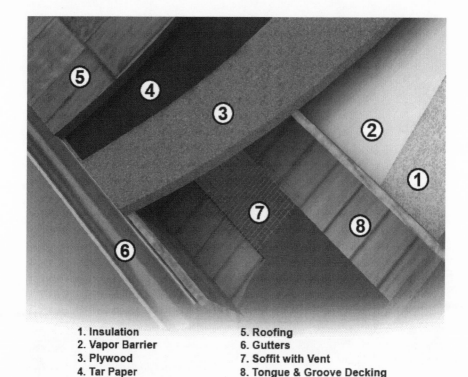

1. Insulation
2. Vapor Barrier
3. Plywood
4. Tar Paper

5. Roofing
6. Gutters
7. Soffit with Vent
8. Tongue & Groove Decking

Weather-Tight Log Homes

The insulating properties of the walls of a log home differ dramatically from those of a conventionally framed home. In a conventional home, walls contain insulation made from a synthetic material. The insulation is covered on the interior with a vapor barrier and some sort of paneling and on the exterior with plywood, tar paper, and then the final exterior layer (such as siding or stucco). Each of these elements contributes to the weather-tightness of the home.

On a log home, the solid log alone separates the interior from the ambient environment outside. The log wall is solid wood—except for the butt joints, corner joints, and the point at which one log rests on the one below it. These horizontal joints constitute the greatest point of concern in making a log home weather-tight, as they are the largest lateral joints through which exterior air or water can enter or interior air can leave.

You can seal butt-and-corner joints against air or water infiltration with a spline system and caulk. Apply a small amount of caulk along these joints as the home is constructed, and then insert a spline, consisting of a strip of steel, plastic, or wood, along the juncture as a final seal. Many log-home manufacturers and builders use readily available wood dowels as splines. Some companies will notch the ends of the logs to allow a large wood spline to be inserted into the slots. Others will use a solid mortise-and-tenon system at the corner joints to facilitate a tight seal. The butt-and-corner joints do not allow as much of area for leakage as the horizontal plane of the logs, but they must be addressed just the same.

The horizontal surface along which one log course lays atop another log course is especially critical. The sealing of this part of a log home must be properly addressed or problems can result over the home's lifetime.

Let's begin with the most basic form of log used in wall construction: one that is flat along its top and bottom without any other sealing system incorporated into the log. The most direct way to seal such a horizontal joint is to apply a copious amount of caulk or chinking on the top surface of the log prior to laying the next course on top. This forms a thin seal that will be only minimally adequate until shrinkage, twisting, or some other movement of the logs occurs over time. If and when this type of movement happens, the original seal separates, and chinking the exterior of the logs becomes necessary to separate the outside climate from the interior one. When the gaps are large enough to warrant the effort, chinking the horizontal joints from inside the house helps as well.

A second method of sealing horizontal joints is to cut a matching groove in the top and bottom of the logs and insert plywood splines. Doing so can prevent air movement between the logs, but it is less successful at preventing water infiltration. Spline grooves should be cut closer to the exterior of the logs rather than to the center, a precaution that keeps moisture away from the interior of the log and guards against decay. This spline system can also use caulk and chinking as backup sealants along the horizontal log joints.

Some logs that are milled round or left in their natural condition have concave copes in their bottom sides to allow a snug fit over the logs below. Between the two rows of logs, a gasket system is used as a final seal. Some companies also recommend chinking such logs on the exterior, both as a seal and for aesthetic appeal.

Yet another system separates each row of logs with a polystyrene seal, such as a one-inch-thick piece of polystyrene sandwiched between two rows of logs. Chinking is then applied along the interior and exterior edges of this polystyrene barrier for both a tight seal and aesthetic appeal. You will also sometimes see this done on some dovetail-style logs on the market.

One of the most frequently used sealing systems is a tongue and groove (T&G) milled into the tops and bottoms of the logs. This can be either a single T&G, a double T&G, or in some cases even a triple T&G. The width and height of such a system can vary widely from one manufacturer to another, and it is normally backed up with some type of gasket material sitting on the top of each tongue. Some manufacturers will cut the groove in the bottom of the logs a bit deeper than the tongue's height to result in a tight seal without the gasket holding the logs apart. In some cases, the manufacturer will mill a drip edge into the lower, exterior edge of the log to allow rain to drip off and not seep in between the logs.

Remember: water and wood do not mix. Keep the logs dry, and be sure that a good sealing system is inherent in the home's design. We previously discussed the importance of adequate overhangs on the roof to keep rain and snow away from the log walls. Logs that are thoroughly seasoned will be more stable than unseasoned logs and result in walls that are less likely to warp, shift, and develop gaps over time. If you use unseasoned logs, be sure to follow the manufacturer's guidelines carefully to allow for proper settling and a resultant adequate seal.

In addition to ensuring properly sealed walls on a log home, you must properly install windows and doors to prevent infiltration by air and water. This is done by sealing around the windows before any trim is installed. Flashing should also be installed over the frames of windows and doors so that rain will not seep in. This flashing is inserted into a slot cut into the log above the window and is then bent over the top of the window frame. Some builders use caulk or chinking over the windows as a seal, but flashing will result in a reliable long-term seal that will not leak.

Whatever type of log home you decide to build, start by choosing the log style that appeals to you, and then make certain that the logs are sealed correctly during construction. Be sure to inform your contractor about the manufacturer's recommended procedure for installing and sealing the logs. In this way, you can ensure that your log home will be not only energy efficient but also long lasting.

Windows and Doors

After you install the windows and doors and before you install the interior trim, you should make the window-to-log and door-to-log connections weather-tight. This is done by spraying expanding foam into the area where each window or door jamb meets the log ends and in the gap between the window and the jamb. This will make an airtight seal around the windows and doors. Merely cut off the excess foam, and you are ready to install the interior window trim. A word of caution: if you are building with unseasoned logs that require months of drying and settling, you had better skip this process until all of the shrinkage and settling has taken place, as this adhesive foam could jeopardize the settling of the logs. Contact your log supplier for the requirements for shrinkage and settling.

Caring for Your Log Home

Chapter Highlights

- Cleaning your log home is important to its appearance and longevity.

- Maintenance of interior and exterior logs is key to the durability of your log home.

Cleaning Wood

If building your home has taken longer than expected, the logs can fade or turn a silver gray. This last stage of the aging process is the worst-case scenario, as it belies the fact that something has gone wrong in the building process. If the logs sit in the weather over an extended period of time, black stains can develop on them. This is caused by rain running over spikes, causing a black iron sulfide stain to streak the logs. After the roof is on and the logs are protected, attention should be turned to these problem areas.

To bring the logs back to a pristine condition, you or your builder can mix 50 percent water and 50 percent household bleach in a pump sprayer and spray down the logs on the exterior and interior. As the logs become gray, you need to use a stronger solution. You could apply a mixture of oxalic acid and water to the logs using a garden sprayer. This brightens the wood and also removes rust stains caused by nails and screws.

Caution: When spraying any chemicals on the logs, wear goggles, gloves, and a long-sleeved shirt. Be extremely careful. If you don't know what you are doing, hire a professional.

After the logs are sprayed on the inside of the home, a raised-grain effect will appear. You will need to sand a little longer and be more diligent when this happens. After you apply the first coat of interior varnish to the logs and let it dry thoroughly, sand the logs again with very fine sandpaper or steel wool to remove the "whiskers" that result after the first coat of finish. Then give it another coat. Don't skimp on this procedure, as a finely finished log will be there forever as a mark of your or your builder's expertise.

What about an insecticide for the exterior wood finish? Some homeowners or builders will add one to the finish to deter carpenter bees or any local wood-boring insects. This material is available from your local hardware store or home center. It certainly won't hurt, but it is not commonly done. Do not use any of these materials for the interior of the home. If you are in an area where termites are a problem, have a local exterminating company treat the soil surface around the house to keep these critters at bay. If you have hand-peeled logs with some bark still on them, using an insecticide in your exterior wood treatment would be wise because insects can be attracted to bark, especially if the logs are unseasoned.

Interior Wood Finishing

There are many interior finishes for log walls. However, most people use a urethane finish. If the logs are unseasoned, you will have to wait for the drying process to run its course before finishing the logs. With dry logs and lumber, the finishing process can begin whenever the roof is on the home. The finish should be delayed until most of the construction is complete so that the finished logs are not damaged by ongoing construction.

Prior to finishing a milled log, sand the interior smooth to remove any stains or bleaching by the sun that took place during construction. If black stains are apparent on the interior of the wall from water running over the spikes or nails and then down the wall, they should be removed before sanding. These stains are generally from iron sulfide, which occurs when rain comes into contact with metal. These are the same black stains that result when ungalvanized nails are used on the exterior of the home. The stains can be removed by mixing warm water and wood bleach, available in most home centers. Rub this water and wood bleach mixture on the stains, and, presto, they disappear.

If you use a belt or palm sander for sanding the interior walls, use a fairly fine grit and keep the sander moving so that you won't dig into the walls. A belt sander will only work with flat interior logs. You will have to sand round logs by hand. Be sure to remove the sanding dust before finishing the logs, or you will have a rough, gritty final finish.

A sanding sealer is used as a first coat because it is less expensive than varnish, and it will seal the logs so that less varnish is required. If you like a subdued look, then this sanding sealer may be all that you will use. It is up to you. The final coat can be either a gloss or a satin urethane varnish. A gloss can bring out the color in knotty pine or cedar and make a lovely final finish. However, some people think that it is too shiny, and they opt for a satin finish. If you use a satin finish, you must periodically stir the finish as you apply it, or the chemicals will settle out and you will get a gloss finish.

There are two types of urethane finishes on the market. One is oil based and will produce an odor in that could give some people a headache in an enclosed space such as a home. The other is a water-based product that does not smell like the oil-based finish. Consider this before buying.

There are many other finishes on the market, and many are available from log-home suppliers. There are so many finishes that covering all of them here is impossible, so you should ask suppliers what they have available. Some finishes are available with a stain already in them, so if a stain is in your future, check these out. The color of the stain on your home may look different than the color on the sample card at the store. Before deciding on a color, get an actual sample from the supplier; then, try the finish on a piece of an extra log. Wait for it to dry, and see if it meets the aesthetic criteria of all those involved in the project.

Exterior Treatments

This section on exterior wood finishing is complicated because a plethora of exterior finishes are on the market. Each claims to be better than the others, and thus entering the arena of wood finishes without any experience in wood finishing, wood protection, or wood preservation is daunting for the homeowner. Most people read the manufacturer's literature and then make a selection. Over the years, we have done "stake" tests on wood finishes to determine which lasts the longest, fades, or peels. This is done by putting one coat of wood finish on a piece of log or log siding and then placing it in the sun and weather without any shelter. This accelerated test will "separate the men from the boys" in a much shorter time than putting two or three coats on a log and placing it in a protected space. What a difference between the brands!

Let us give you basic facts about exterior wood treatments. First, there are no magic bullets in this arena of wood finishing. When you see outlandish claims about ten-year or twenty-year guarantees, lifetime treatment, or a secret formula, beware.

Second, there are no true wood preservatives on the market today as in years past. Concentrated wood preservatives such as Pentachlorophenol (Penta) or Copper Chromate of Arsenate (CCA) have been taken off the market by the Environmental Protection

Agency (EPA) due to the health hazards that they imposed. So when you see "wood preservative" marked on the can, don't think that you have found the magic elixir.

If you want to keep your logs looking natural with the grain showing under their new sheen, then you can use a linseed oil-based exterior finish. The finishes usually consist of linseed oil, mineral spirits, a drying agent, and an ultraviolet light screener. There are many of these in stores today. Several coats are required to put a water-repellent finish on the logs and leave them looking natural. The problem with any exterior finish that builds up on the surface is that the sun will eventually cause peeling. This can turn into a lot of extra work. If that doesn't bother you, then you can mix your own and save money. Mix one to two gallons of mineral spirits into five gallons of boiled linseed oil, and you have basically the same product.

Be aware that the above mixture is fine for dry climates with little or no humidity. If you use this formula in humid areas, then you must add a mildewcide to the mixture. This is available at most home centers or paint stores. It is usually a heavy paste material. Put the recommended amount in the mixture and mix very, very well. We recommend that you dilute it with a quart of the wood treatment material before pouring it into the final batch. Then, stir it for several minutes with a mixing paddle on an electric drill. If this treatment is not added, a black mildew will form on the exterior of the logs during warm, humid months. With any product such as this, make sure that it contains a mildewcide to prevent problems.

When you are reapplying the finish, knock off the peeling finish. There are many ways to do this. Most people use a wire brush, also called an Osborne brush. Others use a high-pressure water blaster to remove the old stain. To completely remove the old stain, log-home owners use a sand blaster filled with corncob media. This is an excellent method to prepare the home for a variety of reasons. First, no water is involved, so stain can be applied immediately after blasting. Second, no harmful chemicals are used, and corncob media is biodegradable. Finally, the corncob blasting creates an excellent surface for the stain to adhere to.

A number of stains, which some people prefer over a natural finish, are available. The homeowner can pick from a multitude of colors. The logs will eventually obtain a brown patina, so homeowners who want to keep their log homes as bright and shiny as the day they were built have an uphill battle ahead. By choosing a stain, they can pick a color that will remain stable for many years. Light woods tend to darken over time, and dark woods tend to lighten. Over many years, with little or no treatment, all woods will turn gray or even black if left to the whims of nature. When the logs turn gray, it is a wake-up call that the wood is beginning to deteriorate. Thus, you must be responsible and take care of your investment as you would your car, lawn, or trees.

Stains can be either transparent or semitransparent. The transparent stain will allow more of the wood grain to show through than the semitransparent stain. A stain treatment will last longer than a clear finish. The stains have particulates in them that give them their color. These particulates also reflect the ultraviolet light, which causes the wood to discolor.

When a penetrating stain is used on the exterior of the logs, a peeling problem will not develop, unlike with finishes that build up on the surface, such as linseed oil or some commercial log oils. As the years go by, the stain will lighten, after which time you need to apply one or more coats. This is far easier than brushing off the peeling wood finish or using a high-pressure water pump to remove the old finish. You merely cover all windows and doors and then spray or brush on another coat of finish.

Some stains are so thick that they resemble paint more than stain. Because the wood grain will be well covered, thick stains are not as popular as light stains. Again, if these are so thick that they build up on the surface, they could have a tendency to peel, especially on the south side of the home (in the northern hemisphere), where heat build-up can become a problem.

Varnishes should not be used on the exterior, as they have a tendency to peel. Limit these finishes to the interior of the log home. With all of the stains and finishes available at the hardware store or building centers, you need to ask questions, try them on a sample of wood before buying, and follow the directions recommended by the manufacturer.

Earlier, we mentioned that wood preservatives are no longer available to homeowners. The oil-based wood preservatives have been removed from the market due to their toxicity. A number of years ago, however, a new preservative manufactured from borate compounds was made available. It can be sprayed on the logs prior to applying the final stain or exterior coating. The drawback to this wood preservative is that it is water-soluble, and thus the dry wood preservative is mixed with water and then sprayed onto the logs. If you have a problem with blowing rain or a leaking gutter, this same compound can be leached from the wood and its effectiveness greatly diminished. This is the reason that this water-soluble wood preservative is not used on pressure-treated lumber, fence posts, and so on. You can use it, but remember not to get sloppy with your maintenance schedule. We place a lot of faith in the mechanical methods—roof overhangs, porches, and a foundation that has adequate clearance between the soil surface and the subfloor—of protecting your logs from the elements.

Threats to Your Home

Chapter Highlights

- Contrary to popular opinion, fire is not the main threat to your log home.

- Proper maintenance and wood treatment can prevent decay.

- Insects can be controlled through proper application of insecticides and common-sense strategies.

Fire

A relative or friend who wants to help with your home-buying decision may tell you that a log home will burn easily, hot, and quickly. Nothing could be farther from the truth. Let's examine the burning qualities of wood, especially of large logs.

Compare kindling that you use to start your fireplace to a large log. Wood with a large cross section will be more difficult to ignite and burn than wood with a small cross section. When starting a fire in your stove or fireplace, the normal sequence of events is to use small kindling to get a small fire started. When this is burning well, you add larger pieces to the fire until, finally, the largest pieces of wood are added, which will keep the fire going for hours. A forest fire starts with the easily ignited duff, which is composed of needles, leaves, and twigs. It does not start by someone holding a match to the side of a standing tree or a log.

At home shows, we used to bring a one-foot piece of log that had been subjected to a propane torch for fifteen minutes. There was a charred spot on the log the size of a silver dollar and one-eighth-inch deep. When the propane torch was taken away from the log, the flame went out, as this large piece of wood would not hold a flame. There wasn't enough surface area to provide the kindling needed to start and maintain a fire. Try it (taking all safety precautions, of course), and you will see what we re talking about.

Fire resistance ratings for walls and floors are based on the standard fire test ASTM E119. This test has three failure criteria, which impact the spread of a fire within a structure:

1. Flame penetration
2. Having an excessive temperature rise on the side of the wall that is not exposed to the fire
3. Failure of the wall to support the full allowable load of the assembly

Studies conducted in the United States and in other countries have found that the log wall tested would withstand the one-hour fire rating. The new *"ICC Standard on the Design and Construction of Log Structures"* includes a prescriptive provision that log walls with a minimum horizontal thickness of 6 inches or greater are equivalent to one-hour fire rated construction. In tests conducted by the National Bureau of Standards (now NIST), a 3-5/8-inch thick non-load-bearing wall lasted 85 minutes, and a 5-1/2- inch-thick non-load-bearing wall lasted 126 minutes. Both walls were constructed of nominal 2-inch thick lumber laid horizontally in a flatwise and nailed together in a manner similar to a log wall. The U.S. Forest Products Laboratory tested a 7.5-inch-thick nail laminated wood wall with plain joints (not tongue-and-groove joints), and the uncharred wood remaining after 2.3 hours was 3.91 inches thick. In recognition of their inherent fire resistance, the 2003 International Urban-Wildland Interface Code specifically excluded heavy timber and log wall construction from requirements that the exterior walls be of one-hour fire resistance-rated construction. The 2001 or later editions of the National Design Specification for Wood Construction include a methodology for determining the fire resistance rating of exposed wood members.

In a frame home (some 80 percent of all home construction is of this type), the framing of the home is composed of two-by-fours or two-by-sixes in the wall. These are spaced 16 to 24 inches apart. The two-by-ten or two-by-twelve joists are likewise spaced 16 inches on center and covered with plywood or oriented strandboard. When a fire starts in the basement or some other area where the framing is not covered with gypsum board, these small members carry the fire easily, as they are small in comparison to logs. A log home has the same type of subfloor, but the logs, second-floor joists, and possibly the beam rafters are large. Getting these large wood members to catch fire and spread through the home takes longer than the smaller studs and plywood in a conventional home.

We have seen several log homes catch fire during our careers in the log-home industry. In two cases, the fire started in the basement; one fire was caused by electrical problems, and the other stemmed from a problem with a wood furnace or stove in the basement. In both cases, the fire got a good start in fuel located in the basement. It then burned out the first-floor joists, the second-floor system, and finally the roof. After the structural members were consumed, the log walls finally caught fire and fell into the basement to be consumed as a large, hot fire.

The use of metal in building construction can give one a false sense of security. Of course, the metal will not burn, but the contents of the building will. The heat from the burning contents will significantly decrease the strength of steel I beams, and then the structure will collapse. This is essentially what happened to the "fireproof" McCormack Center in Chicago back in the late 1960s. When the metal structural members lost their strength, the building lost its structural integrity.

The exterior log wall or wood siding of a home can be impregnated or coated with chemicals that will increase its resistance to fire. Such treatments are designed to reduce the spread of flames on the surface of the wood. With log homes in timbered settings, such treatments of the exterior surfaces may be warranted. There may be questions about the durability of the treatment, particularly for the coatings. A better approach would be to cut the trees and brush back from around the house to maintain a defensive space around your home. This will not only help to keep the exterior of the logs ventilated to prevent decay but also to reduce the risk of a wildfire spreading to the home. Visit Web sites such as www.firewise.org for additional ideas on how to protect your home in a timbered setting.

In this same regard, a Class-A fire-rated roof may be warranted. Fire-rated roofs are classified as A, B, or C. Class A is the highest rating. Embers carried by the wind will be less likely to cause damage to a fire-rated roof than to an unrated cedar shake roof.

A few clients over the years have told us that certain insurance companies did not want to insure a log home for fire. These instances are rare indeed. We hear of this so rarely that we never give it a second thought when we talk to potential log-home buyers.

Decay

Decay in wood is caused by contact with fungal spores. In the right conditions (temperature, moisture content, and oxygen supply), these spores can turn into fungus. A fungus is a microscopic plant that sends threadlike roots called haustoria into the wood. These haustoria excrete enzymes that dissolve the cellulose and lignin of the wood and use it for food.

In very hot or cold conditions, fungi, like many other plants, will not grow]. Temperatures below 50°F and above 90°F are not suitable for the growth of fungi. Thus, in most parts of the United States, fungi can grow four to six months a year, and more than that in the south. A fungus grows when the humidity is between 30 and 60 percent.

Needless to say, you cannot limit oxygen around your home to deter fungus, so you can skip that method of control. You also cannot limit the temperature, so you can forget that too. So, let's look at moisture content.

Fungi do not thrive in extremely moist or extremely dry areas, but you cannot and do not want to keep your logs wet by spraying them with a constant mist of water. You can, however, keep the logs and all of your lumber dry. To do this, we return to our previous discussions on large roof overhangs, rain gutters, and downspouts. By having a large space of concrete foundation between the soil surface and the subfloor, you can minimize rain splash. This last construction tip is of utmost concern in all homes. You can build a home of stone, but if you a subfloor rots, you will be in trouble, and the house will fall in a heap in due time. The porch floors should be made from resistant woods such as heartwood of western red cedar, redwood, cypress or from pressure-treated lumber. Normally, the pressure-treated lumber available today is CCA treated. This can be either the standard green material or ordered in a color such as brown to fit in with the log home.

You must keep the outside of the log home covered with a water-repellent finish. This should be done when it begins to fade. Try to the following test: Throw a glass of water on the logs. If the water soaks into the logs instead of beading up and running off, it is time to recoat the logs. A stain may keep the logs looking good to the eye, but they will lose their water repellency in time. Make sure that your rain gutters and downspouts are clean of foreign matter and that they do not overflow during a rainstorm. Also, have pipes attached to the downspouts so that the water is directed away from the foundation.

If you see green mold on the exterior of the logs, then the logs are receiving too much moisture from rain. If this happens, you need to obtain a water-soluble wood preservative from a log-home supplier and soak the logs with it. If you have taken care in building and designing your log home with the construction tips covered earlier, mold should not be a problem. Remember, for rot to occur, the moisture content of the wood must be between 30 and 60 percent. That type of moisture requires extensive and periodic wettings. With minimal overhangs and a lack of rain gutters and downspouts, this can happen in the humid parts of the United States.

There is no such thing as "dry rot." Dry rot refers to the dry, crumbly nature of the rot when it has progressed past the point of no return. All rot requires moisture to progress to the point where it is deleterious to the structure. If you are in an arid or semiarid part of the country, be cautious about sprinkling your lawn to keep the grass green. I have seen logs rot because the in-ground sprinkler system shot copious quantities of water against the log home on a regular basis. It sounds like a dumb thing to do, but most of us don't keep an eye on the sprinkler when it is on, and many people don't have a clue about wood and what it takes to begin the rotting cycle.

We encourage you to keep shrubs away from your log home. Shrubs and bushes will create a barrier of high humidity if they are planted close to the log home. Furthermore, they will deflect rain onto the logs, causing the logs to remain wet for an extended period of time, which will encourage mold, spores, and possibly rot. One of us received a call from a woman who complained about rotting logs on the existing log home she had purchased. From an office over a thousand miles away, we told her that she probably had shrubs planted too close to the house and didn't have a rain gutter. She was amazed because those were the exact conditions that led to her problems.

The point is that you need to keep the logs dry with proper construction, timely maintenance, and installation of rain gutters and downspouts. This also pertains to conventional, stick-framed construction, but it is very often neglected by homeowners, architects, and engineers. In this day of space-age and low-maintenance materials in everything from cars to homes, it is no wonder that people run afoul of basic, common-sense principles of design and maintenance.

Insects

When we mention insects in connection with log homes, people get paranoid. They visualize swarms of insects heading for their new log homes like clouds of locusts. I have been in the log-home manufacturing business for over thirty years and have never seen a termite problem in a log home. Certainly, there are cases of termites getting into the logs, but we are sure that this was due mainly to poor construction. There are other insects that can cause problems, but in many cases they arrived in logs that were improperly stored at the mill or infested the logs when they were on the job site for a long time without adequate protection.

Termites

Termites, sometimes called white ants, are social insects. They are related to cockroaches rather than to ants. A termite can be distinguished from an ant by the absence of a narrow waist on its body and its typically white color. Under a hand lens, termite antennae are straight, whereas those of ants have an elbow. Flying reproductive termites, called alates, can be distinguished from flying ants by the equal size of all four termite wings.

Subterranean Termites

The subterranean termite is the most destructive termite in the United States. They are prevalent in the southeastern United States where it is warm and damp. These two factors are why you will not find them much in the northern United States. The termites live in colonies in the soil and attack wood that is in close proximity to their colonies. To get into a home, they build a tunnel up the side of the foundation. This tunnel also serves to bring moisture up with them so that they can survive. This method of travel makes a termite shield an attractive deterrent to termite infestation. A metal lip sticking past the top of the foundation foils their tunnel-building activities.

Termites pose the most risk to homes that are built on a slab (close proximity to the soil surface) and to homes that are built on a crawl space (poorly ventilated, damp, and in close proximity to the soil surface). Any support posts located in the basement or crawl space should be metal (adjustable lolly columns) or pressure-treated wood. Heartwood from redwood can be a deterrent, but it doesn't work as well as pressure-treated wood.

Formosan Termite

This termite was inadvertently transported to the United States after WWII when equipment was brought back from the Far East after hostilities ended. This pest is a native of East Asia and now inhabits a number of southern states, but it is not found beyond these states. You should determine if this termite is located in your area before taking precautions to prevent infestations. There is nothing additional you can do to keep these termites out of your building that you haven't already done to deter other termites. If they become established in an existing building or are particularly bad around your property, contact a professional to treat the soil and crawl space or to fumigate the building.

The Formosan termite is much less destructive than the subterranean termite discussed earlier. This is partly due to its limited range. They do not need to build tunnels to gain access to a home or building. Thus, it is easier for them to move around. Use the same precautions as mentioned earlier; in particular, treat the soil surface to destroy any colonies living in the soil and to deter future colonies.

Insects, such as termites, cannot smell the large mass of wood, so they will not deliberately fly to it and begin the process of devouring your home.

Prevention

In the case of termites, keep waste wood, wood shavings, and other loose wood away from your home. Wood buried or partially buried makes an ideal home for termites. Once established, they will continue to cause problems until they are exterminated.

Have your soil treated periodically around the perimeter of the foundation by a reliable pest-control company. Keep the foundation well above the soil surface, twelve to eighteen inches, as mentioned

Subterranean termites. Photo by Scott Bauer, courtesy of USDA Agricultural Research Service.

earlier. Install a termite shield between the foundation and the sill plate of the home. The sill plate should be made of pressure-treated material. In areas of high humidity or termite infestation, the exterior rim joists (box sill) should be pressure treated as well. Finally, the joists should be pressure treated if you have a damp crawl space. The crawl space should be free of waste wood and have a plastic vapor barrier to keep moisture from condensing on the floor joists and plywood.

Spend extra money on these items now, and you will be worry-free in a home that can be resold years later. Don't listen to those who say that such precautions are not required by code. Build it right, and you can sleep at night knowing that your dream home will not be degraded by insects or moisture.

Carpenter Ants

Carpenter ants are large ants (1/4" to 1" in length) that are indigenous to many parts of North America. Carpenter ants can enter the home on their own volition, or they can be carried in with firewood or other materials. They can be either black or brown; they are large ants (up to one inch in length), so when you see one you will know it. To deter these ants, follow the guidelines discussed above for termites. Be careful about stacking firewood in and around the home. Some years back, we got a call from a log-home owner who had ants crawling around his house. It didn't take long for him to bring out the fact that he had old firewood stacked near the fireplace. He cleaned this out of the home, and the problem was eliminated. In another case, a couple had carpenter ants in their home. After questioning them, one of us found out that they had built on property infested with carpenter ants. It was easy to prescribe a pest control company to fumigate the home and treat the soil surface over an extensive area around the home.

Carpenter ant. Photo courtesy of Clemson University, USDA Cooperative Extension Slide Series.

Prevention

Damage from carpenter ants. Photo by Joseph O'Brien, courtesy of USDA Forest Service.

The recipe to avert problems here is proper construction, soil treatment, and common sense about bringing old firewood into the home. Insects in your home are usually the result of skipping some of the construction principles that we have outlined.

Insects/Larva

If the logs are improperly stored at the mill, insects can become established under the bark. If logs with bark are used, insects can continue to inhabit the logs.

Insect larvae. Photo courtesy of Clemson University, USDA Cooperative Extension Slide Series

Prevention

During the construction phase, keep all lumber covered with tarps or plastic, and keep the materials off of the ground. We seldom find materials properly covered from the elements or off the soil when we visit job sites. It seems that people have forgotten how to take care of wood since we've entered the synthetic age of plastic and vinyl. We are repeating this same theme over and over so that it will stick in the minds of new homeowners.

Powder Post Beetle. Photo courtesy of USDA Forest Service Archives.

Never place lumber in your home if the material has active insect borings. If you see these, discard the material and replace it with material that is free from any evidence of insect activity. This is especially important if you find insects or traces of boring marks under the bark of your logs. If you hear a borer in the wood after construction, find out exactly from where the sound is coming. If you find the entrance hole, you can fill it with insecticide to kill the inhabitant. If the problem is extensive, consult a pest-control company for advice and/or treatment.

Powder Post Beetles (Old House Borers)

Powder post beetles can infect lumber and wood materials before the log home is constructed. This usually happens when the lumber is still wet or partially seasoned. The eggs are laid, and the adults leave the structure upon completing their lifecycles. The exit holes are very small, in the neighborhood of one-eighth to one-sixteenth inches in diameter.

Small holes are evidence that powder post beetles inhabit your lumber or logs. If there are active beetles in the wood, you will find sawdust coming out of the holes. These can be treated on a small scale with insecticide, but if a great deal of infestation is apparent, contact a pest-control company.

Some powder post beetles inhabit and eat hardwood only, while others prefer softwood such as pine. If wood is kiln dried at a high heat and low humidity and to a low moisture content, these insects can be killed in the wood members. If they are merely kiln dried to rid the wood of most of its free water without getting the wood really hot and bringing the moisture down to low levels, then the insects can remain alive.

Damage from powder post beetles.
Photo by Gyorgy Csoka, courtesy of Hungary Forest Research Institute.

Carpenter Bees

Carpenter bee. Photo by Jerry A. Payne,
courtesy of USDA Agricultural Research Service.

In some areas, carpenter bees can attack dry, seasoned lumber or logs. They bore a hole into the wood about one-half inch in diameter and set up house. To kill them, you can spray an insecticide into the hole during the night when they inhabit the burrow. These bees are not a big problem, but they do surface periodically. Their nests can attract woodpeckers, which eat the bees and the larvae.

Most of the insects covered above can be taken care of by a locally applied insecticide. If for some reason they persist or are found in large populations, contact a pest-control company. We do not want to give specifics as to insecticides, as what is available today can be taken off the market in the future. If insect infestation were a big problem in log homes, we would cover it in greater detail; however, this is not the case. Most problems are caused by poor construction, low-grade building materials, or a localized anomaly that can usually be taken care of with household insecticides and common sense.

Evaluating and Purchasing an Existing Log Home

Chapter Highlights

- Consider using an organized checklist when evaluating an existing log home for purchase. Items such as location, condition, construction techniques, and finishes will impact your life in the home.

- Shrinkage and weather-tightness are crucial items to consider. Ensure that your future home has been well maintained and its systems are in place.

Americans are very mobile. They move for a change of climate, for a new job, or for retirement and a new lifestyle. The result of this constant change of scene is that homes come up for sale. If you are interested in purchasing an existing log home and skipping the many steps required to build your own log home, then it is time to contact a realtor and ask about available log homes.

The Basics

To begin with, you should look at and evaluate any home during foul weather and not on a warm, quiet day. If it is cold and raining with a stiff wind, you can find the weak spots in a home quickly. Bring a checklist of items to look for, and don't be sidetracked by the décor or furnishings or what the realtor wants to highlight. Talk little and look a lot. Idle conversation can distract you from the construction and maintenance points that need to be checked carefully. Let's begin!

First, you will want to keep mental track of how far you are from a grocery store, hospital, the nearest town, and your job. We have had clients who wanted to get out into the country but, after a few years, got tired of driving to town and their jobs and sold their homes. You must be practical in this regard. If your children are still in school, you may get tired of driving them to all of their activities if you live some distance from the school or town.

Roads and Access

As you drive to the home, note the conditions of the county roads. How will they be maintained in the winter? Are the roads gravel, or are they paved? How is the drainage next to the road? Are there low-water bridges that become impassable during summer rains? If a tree blows down or an ice storm hits the area, are you likely to lose power because the trees are growing next to the utility lines?

Look carefully at the driveway. If it is unpaved, will it get soft and rutted during rains, or (in northern climates) will it soften when the frost goes out? Will ditches next to the driveway allow plenty of drainage during summer storms? And, finally, how will drifting snow affect the driveway?

Exterior

When you arrive at the home, you should not go directly into the home and get sidetracked by the floor plan and the interior décor. Check the exterior of the home for any degradation that may have resulted over the years. If the home is fairly new, the effects of poor construction or low-quality materials may not have become apparent at this early stage.

Have the logs had any shrinkage since the home was built? This can be determined as spaces between each successive course of logs and possibly some twisting of the logs.

If caulk or chinking has been applied at some selected spots, then there may be some sort of leaking problem. Do not confuse a log home that has been chinked completely as one that is a problem home. Some people chink their homes inside and out to give the rustic appearance of a log home of years gone by. This is a normal procedure on many of the dovetailed log homes or the saddle-notched log homes. This was the norm in traditional log homes in the West and in the Appalachians. Thus, this chinking applied to the entire home is for aesthetic appeal and not a shot at correcting a problem.

Has the home been refinished lately, or has it been left to weather naturally with the logs suffering from rot? How is the finish on the home? Try the test we mentioned earlier: Throw a glass of water onto the logs. If the water soaks quickly into the logs, then they need another application of finish. Do you see a lot of cracks in the exterior of the logs that can collect moisture and result in decay?

Don't forget the inherent design criteria of log construction. There should be adequate roof overhangs, especially in areas of high rainfall. If the overhangs are not adequate, you will notice where rain splash has deposited soil onto the bottom courses of logs. If the homeowner has planted shrubs close to the log walls, this can also be a problem. Rain can be deflected onto the log walls by these shrubs, causing the logs to rot. Furthermore, the shrubs can slow down the drying process when the weather clears, resulting in decay.

Check the clearance between the soil surface and the top of the foundation; if it is less than a foot, problems can result. If the home has a porch, you should check the bottom of the porch posts to see if you can spot signs of rot. A problem can be detected if the posts are moldy, have any plant or fungus growing from them, or are heavily cracked. The porch deck can also show these signs if it is not built from pressure-treated or rot-resistant lumber.

Interior

Finally, you enter the log home. Does the front door stick, or does it open and close easily without any signs of light coming in around the door? If it is a windy day, you should check for air leaks with a cigarette lighter or match around not only the doors but also the windows. Ask what brand of windows and doors are in the home. If you are not familiar with the brand, ask an employee at a local home center or builder what he or she thinks of them. Are the windows the inexpensive aluminum type, or are they wood-framed with aluminum or vinyl on the exterior to minimize maintenance. If it is a cold day, look to see if any moisture has condensed between the double panes of glass. If the windows are single pane, then you have a cheaper window that is not going to be energy efficient. At this point, alarm bells should be going off, as someone has evidently put substandard materials into the log home.

Also, open the windows to make sure that they are properly installed and open smoothly. If they don't, the header log may be putting undue pressure on the windows, which may eventually cause them to crack. Try the sash locks; they should lock and open freely. Look for stains near or around the windows and doors. If staining is present, this shows that they were improperly installed and that rain has entered.

At this time, look at the logs. Have any shrunk, causing gaps to appear between individual log courses? Have the logs been caulked or chinked here and there to fix problems. Again, look for staining of the logs where rain has come through a crack. Many times, these stains will be black where they come in contact with the spikes or lag screws. Check the corners for air leakage with a match or cigarette lighter. If the home has a loft, check for air leaks where the gable ends come into contact with the tongue and groove on the roof. If the gable is constructed of log siding and tongue-and-groove lumber, check for air leaks here as well. If the gable was built without roofer's felt and plywood, air leakage can become a problem.

If the home has wood floors, make sure that they fit tightly together and didn't suffer shrinkage due to lower-grade materials or from getting wet during the construction phase. Ask the realtor what type of flooring it is; is it hardwood or is it soft pine? Has the finish become worn so that it will have to be sanded and refinished? This would be another expense after you purchase the home.

There are many more items that we could add, but the list will vary with the age and type of log home that you are buying. Be alert, and look carefully. Ask plenty of questions, and have the seller provide you with a disclaimer if you are concerned about any particular items.

With log homes being built by all sorts of builders and do-it-yourself carpenters, the construction quality can range from excellent to miserable. The points that we have brought up should not make you think that buying a log home is a crapshoot but rather a risk that can be managed with thorough inspection. If you have any concerns about the home that the seller does not answer, consult an expert—an engineer, forester, architect, or an employee of a local home centers. Be a careful buyer, and enjoy your log home!

Buying an Existing Log Home Checklist

- ✓ General Location
    - o Consider the distance from:
        - ▪ Hospitals
        - ▪ Grocery stores
        - ▪ Movies
        - ▪ Work
        - ▪ Friends
        - ▪ Children
    - o Consider the road conditions.
        - ▪ Are the roads paved or gravel?
        - ▪ How are the roads in the winter?
- ✓ Exterior
    - o Have the logs been treated recently?
    - o Are there cracks in the exterior face of the logs?
    - o Is shrinkage of the logs apparent?
    - o Has the exterior been chinked to fill in cracks resulting from shrinkage?
    - o Are there adequate overhangs on the roof?
    - o Have rain gutters and downspouts been installed?
    - o Is there adequate clearance between the soil surface and the first logs of the house?
    - o Do the porch and deck show signs of deterioration?
- ✓ Interior
    - o Windows and Doors
        - ▪ Check the exterior doors and windows for sticking.
        - ▪ Use a cigarette lighter to check for air leakage.
        - ▪ What brand of windows and doors are installed in the home?
        - ▪ Is there moisture condensation between the windowpanes of insulated-glass windows?
        - ▪ Do the sash locks engage easily?
        - ▪ Are there stains around windows and doors that show leakage?

- Logs
  - Look for signs of shrinkage between log courses.
  - Check for water stains on the surface of the logs.
  - Has caulk been applied to different spots on the logs to rectify leaking problems?
  - Check for air leakage with a cigarette lighter.
  - Check gable ends for any signs of leakage.

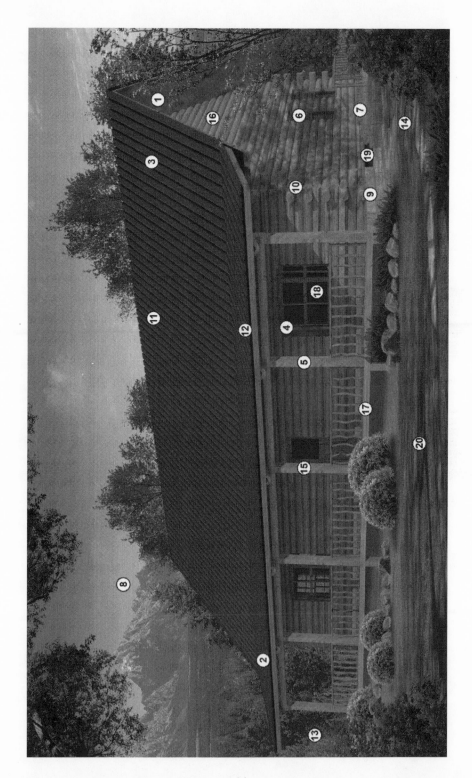

144

20 Highlights of a Well Built Log Home

1. The overhang at the gable ends should have a five-foot overhang to protect the logs from rain, sun, and the elements in general.

2. The slope of a roof is very important. Make sure the roof slope meets the building code for your area. A poorly sloped roof can allow snow and water to accumulate. Having an adequately sloped roof will extend the life of your roof.

3. The roof should be made of quality materials. In forested areas, a metal or fire-resistant material should be used. This kind of high-quality roof can also prevent hail damage.

4. Insulated-glass windows with low-E glass and exterior cladding are best. In high-wind or very cold areas, casements are recommended. Triple glazing should also be considered.

5. Porch posts should be installed up off the floor surface to prevent rotting from the end grain. Tie the porch floor to the piers, and tie the porch posts to the porch floor and the porch roof to prevent failure during high winds.

6. Use metal flashing—not caulk—over windows and doors to keep rain from seeping in over the top of the windows.

7. Keep shrubs away from the house. They can deflect rain to the logs and the lower wood structure. They can also act as shade and keep the logs wet longer after a rain.

8. Remove old or large trees growing close to the house before construction ensues. If they are close to the house, basement excavation can cut the roots and hasten their demise.

9. The top of the foundation should be eighteen inches above the soil surface. This will minimize rain splash hitting the logs and keep

insects at bay. Remember, as a minimum, to put a termite shield on top of the foundation and use a pressure-treated sill plate.

10. The log corners should not protrude too far; eight inches is recommended for logs less than or equal to eight by eight. On larger logs, more overhang is permitted, but extend the roof overhang if the logs stick out beyond eighteen inches.

11. If your log home is going to have a dormer, a two foot minimum over hang should be installed. This will prevent rain splash from hitting the sides of the dormer and causing damage. Flashing should be installed where the dormer materials attach to the main roof.

12. Make sure to install rain gutters and downspouts on your log home. Without rain gutters rain can was down the side of the home staining the wood and finally settling around the foundation causing deterioration.

13. Plant a shelter belt on the north/northwest side of the home to cut down on cold winds and enhance the energy efficiency of the home. Do not plant right next to the home.

14. Slope the driveway away from the garage door to prevent seepage into the garage during heavy rains. Build a solid driveway before the job begins, not after.

15. Use pressure-treated wood for posts exposed to the elements. Use metal end caps at the top to prevent rain from soaking into the end grain. Mount posts off of the concrete.

16. Use water-repellent wood finish on the exterior after construction and periodically as it begins to fade.

17. Use rot-resistant material for the decks and exposed stairs. Do not use raw pine poles for deck railings if they will be exposed to the elements. They will require a great deal of maintenance and will eventually succumb to the elements.

18. Keep large glass windows twelve inches off the deck surface so that snow will not drift over the windows and cause leakage problems both around the windows and between the double panes of glass.

19. Never place logs or log siding right down to the soil surface on a walk-out basement. Use stone to provide an eighteen-inch clearance between the concrete and the first wood.

20. Slope the soil surface away from the home, and provide for adequate drainage so that water will not settle in low spots.

Conclusion

It is said all economic decisions are based on an infinite allocation of scarce resources. Simply stated, there are many items to buy and own, but the limited amount of money that most people have to spend makes a careful allocation of this money a necessity. When you plan to build a home, this rule comes into play at every stage of construction. You may be building your dream home, but unless you have a dream budget, you must monitor and control costs.

By reading about the different log types, fasteners, gaskets, windows, and doors, you can make decisions based on your budget. You can also decide if you really want to build your own home. Remember to ask questions of all people that you deal with so that you will know what you are getting. Finally, get the important items in writing, especially from suppliers. Don't trust the many details of building a home to memory.

An educated shopper will end up with the best product.

Appendices

Appendix A

Table 1 "R" Factors of Some Common Woods	
Bald Cypress	1.20
Douglas Fir (Coastal)*	1.15 /1.27*
Engelmann Spruce	1.52
Loblolly Pine	1.08
Lodgepole Pine	1.30
Ponderosa Pine	1.34
Shortleaf Pine	1.10
Northern White Cedar	1.66
Western Hemlock	1.28
Western Red Cedar	1.56
Northern Red Oak	0.90
Red Pine	1.22
Western White Pine	1.34
Quaking Aspen	1.39
*Rocky Mountain Douglas Fir	
Source: U.S. Forest Products Laboratory	

Appendix B

Percentage of shrinkage from the green to oven-dry condition			
Species	Shrinkage		
	Radial	Tangential	Volumetric
Ponderosa Pine	3.9%	3.9%	12.0
Eastern White Pine	2.1%	2.1%	10.5%
Lodgepole Pine	4.3%	4.3%	6.8%
Western Red Cedar	2.4%	2.4%	9.7%
Coastal Douglas Fir	4.8%	4.8%	8.2%
Loblolly Pine	4.8%	4.8%	11.1%
Bald Cypress	3.8%	3.8%	12.4%
Douglas Fir (Coastal)	4.8%	4.8%	8.2%
Engelmann Spruce	3.8%	7.1%	11.0%
Eastern White Pine	2.1%	2.1%	10.5%
Loblolly Pine	4.8%	4.8%	11.1%
Lodgepole Pine	4.3%	4.3%	6.0%
Ponderosa Pine	3.9%	3.9%	12.0%
Shortleaf Pine	4.6%	7.7%	12.3%
Northern White Cedar	2.2%	4.9%	7.2%
Western Hemlock	4.2%	7.8%	12.4%
Western Red Cedar	2.4%	2.4%	9.7%
Northern White Cedar	2.2%	4.9%	7.2%
Red Pine (Norway)	4.0%	8.6%	13.7%
Western White Pine	4.1%	4.1%	11.8%
Rocky Mountain Douglas Fir (Interior West)	4.8%	7.5%	11.8%
Source: U.S. Forest Products Laboratory			

Appendix C

Tools Required to Build a Log Home

Whether you plan to build the log home by yourself or to hire a contractor, you will need the right tools to complete construction without delays. Oftentimes, a log-home construction job is held up for several hours when a caulking gun or electric drill is not on the job site. A caulking gun is a trivial item, but it is generally required to caulk butt-and-corner joints. With a checklist of tools at your disposal, these untimely delays can be avoided.

Item	Minimum Quantity
Safety glasses, hard hats, gloves	As needed
16-ounce claw hammer	2
8-pound sledgehammer	2
Hand saw	1
Circular saw	1
Drill bits (1½", 5/16", 3/8") and 1½-inch spade bit	1 each
16-foot tape measure	2
30-foot tape measure	1
50-foot tape	1
Belt sander	1
Pinch bar	1
Screwdriver	1
Caulking gun	2
Staple gun	1
First-aid kit	1
Chalk line	1
Framing square	1
Electric power planer	1
Water level	1
3-foot level	1
Hacksaw with extra blades	1

Heavy-duty ½-inch electric drill	1
Electric drill, ¼-inch	1
Saber saw	1
Plunge router	1
Portable scaffolding	As needed
Chainsaw	Optional
Large, 14-inch or 16-inch circular saw	Optional

Appendix D

Basic Cross Section of a Roof System

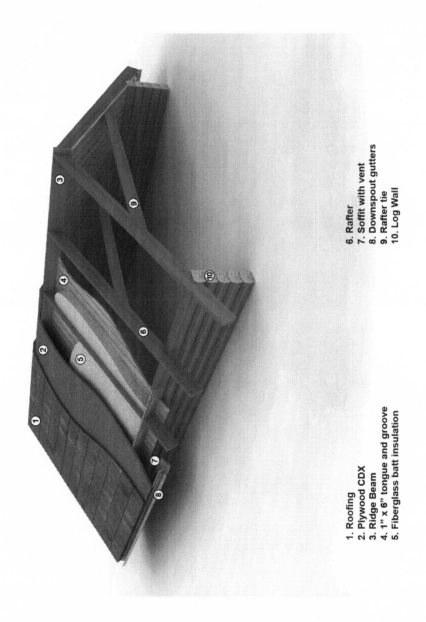

1. Roofing
2. Plywood CDX
3. Ridge Beam
4. 1" x 6" tongue and groove
5. Fiberglass batt insulation

6. Rafter
7. Soffit with vent
8. Downspout gutters
9. Rafter tie
10. Log Wall

Appendix E
Basic Cross Section of a Log Home

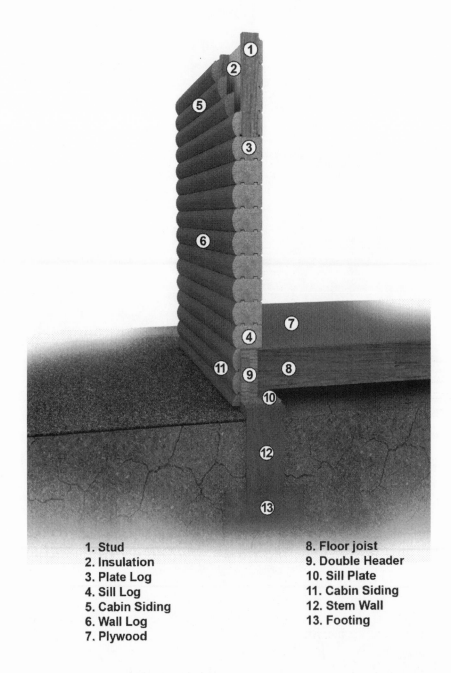

1. Stud
2. Insulation
3. Plate Log
4. Sill Log
5. Cabin Siding
6. Wall Log
7. Plywood
8. Floor joist
9. Double Header
10. Sill Plate
11. Cabin Siding
12. Stem Wall
13. Footing

Glossary

Air-dried wood Wood that is stacked and stickered to allow air to flow between the wood members. The moisture content of air-dried wood is in equilibrium with the relative humidity. This is generally under 17 percent.

Annual growth ring The layer of wood growth put on a tree during a single growing season.

Backfilling Replacing the earth that was removed during excavation around a foundation.

Beam A structural member supporting a load applied transversely to it.

Birdsmouth joint A cut into the end of a timber to fit over a cross timber, usually cut into a rafter.

Board foot The measurement of rough lumber one inch thick, twelve inches wide, and twelve inches long.

Box beam An assembly made by joining layers of lumber together with mechanical fastenings so that the grain of all laminations is essentially equal.

Braces Lumber or timbers placed diagonally between posts and beams or plates to make a structure more rigid.

Cant A log that has been slabbed on one or more sides.

Check A lengthwise separation of the wood that usually extends across the rings of annual growth and commonly results from stresses set up in wood during seasoning.

Collar tie The timber parallel to the girders, which connect rafter pairs at a given height.

Conventional frame Plywood and stud construction.

D An abbreviation used in nail sizes, also referred to as "penny."

Dead load The combined weight of all the materials and all the permanent attachments of a structure.

Decay The decomposition of wood substances by fungi.

Deck A synonym for "floor."

Deflection A bending or sagging.

Density Weight per given unit of volume.

Dormer A vertical window or opening coming through a sloping roof; usually provided with its own pitched roof.
Dressed A board that has been planed smooth.

Dry rot A term loosely applied to any dry, crumbly rot that permits the wood to be crushed easily into a powder. This is a misnomer, as wood must be wet to rot.

Drywall Interior covering materials such as plywood, gypsum, and hardboard.

Face The surface of a board or lumber.

Fire resistance The property of a material or assembly to withstand fire or to give protection from it.

Flashing A strip of usually flexible material that keeps water out of joints between roofs and walls.

Forces Strengths or energies exerted on a building or member.

Framing Lumber used for the structural members of a building such as studs and joists.

Gable roof A sloping roof with one or more triangle-shaped end walls between the rafters.

Gambrel A roof design with a lower, steeper slope and upper, flatter one, designed so that each gable is pentagonal.

Garrison A house design having a second-story perimeter larger than the first story.

Girder A large or principal beam of wood or steel used to support concentrated loads at isolated points along its length.

Grain The direction, size, arrangement, appearance, or quality of the fibers of wood or lumber.

Green Freshly sawed or undried wood.

Half-lap A joint having an L-shaped mortise and a corresponding L-shaped tenon.

Hand-hewn A timber squared off and shaped by hand.

Heartwood The wood extending from the pitch to the sapwood, the cells of which no longer participate in the life process of the tree. Heartwood may contain phenolic compounds, gums, resins, and other materials that usually make it darker and more decay-resistant than sapwood.

Kerf The width of the saw cut.

Knee braces Short, diagonal timbers placed between horizontal and vertical members of the frame to make them rigid.

Knot A place in the tree from which a branch has grown out.

Laminate A product made by bonding together two or more layers of material or materials.

Linear foot A foot measure in a line.

Lintel A small beam over a door, window, or fireplace opening.

Live load A variable load on a structure.

Lumber boards Lumber that is nominally less than two inches thick and two or more inches wide.

Lumber dimension Lumber with a nominal thickness from two inches and up to but not including five inches.

Moisture content The amount of water contained in wood, usually expressed as a percentage of the weight of the oven-dried wood.

On center A method for indicating the spacing of framing members by stating the measurement from the center of the succeeding one.

Plate The horizontal member that supports the rafters.

Preservative Any substance that, for a reasonable time, is effective in preventing the development and action of wood-rotting fungi, borers, and various insects that deteriorate wood.

R-value A number measuring a material's resistance to heat flow. "R" stands for resistance, the inverse of conductivity.

Rafter One of a series of structural members of a roof designed to support roof loads. The rafters of a flat roof are sometimes called joists.

Roof pitch A ratio of the height of the ridge to the span of the building.

Salt box A house design named for its roof, which is composed of two shed roofs having unequal pitches.

Sheathing The first covering of boards or waterproof material on the outside walls and roof.

Slope The degree of deviation from the horizontal or perpendicular. Also, an "incline."

Stringer A timber or other support for cross members in floors or ceilings. In stairs, the stringer is the support in which the stair treads rest.

Structural timbers Large pieces of wood whose strength is the controlling element in their selection and use.

Tail The end portion of a birdsmouth joint, which extends beyond the plate when there is a roof overhang.

Tongue-and-groove An adjective describing boards that fit together edge to edge.

Truss An assembly of members such as beams, bars, or rods combined to form a rigid framework. All members are interconnected to form triangles.

Vapor barrier A watertight material used to prevent the passage of moisture through floors, walls, and ceilings.

Wane Bark or lack of wood from any cause on the ledge or corner of a piece.

Weather-tight A structure that is covered with siding and a roof and that has windows and doors so that it is completely sheltered from the elements.

About the Authors

Clyde Cremer brings a lifetime of expertise to the design and construction of high-quality log homes. He earned an associate degree and a certificate as a forest technician from Lassen College in Susanville, California; a bachelor of science in forestry from Stephen F. Austin University in Nacogdoches, Texas; and a master of forestry degree from the Yale University School of Forestry and Environmental Studies in New Haven, Connecticut. He joined as a charter member and served as a director of the North American Log Builder's Association and was founder and director of the Connecticut Wood Producers Association. Clyde also gained valuable experience in the mid-1970s as an inspector for the Tree Farms Association of Connecticut. In 1977, he founded American Log Homes, where he still serves as president, and he maintains his connection to forestry as a professional member of the Society of American Foresters.

Jeffrey Cremer worked in the family business while growing up, gaining firsthand experience as he helped to build log homes during summer breaks from college. He holds a bachelor of arts degree in sociology from Colorado State University and is studying a master of science in construction management from Arizona State University. Jeff also brings to the log-home business top-notch experience gained while working as a project engineer for one of the largest engineering companies in the world.

About American
Log Homes

No other log-home company offers the dynamic combination of absolute expertise, dedication, quality, and commitment that American Log Homes provides. Company founder and president Clyde Cremer built on his childhood love of nature in rural Iowa to earn a bachelor of science in forestry from Stephen F. Austin State University in Nacogdoches, Texas. He then completed a master of forestry degree from the Yale School of Forestry and Environmental Studies in 1973.

Clyde founded American Log Homes in Missouri in July 1977 and moved its headquarters to Pueblo West, Colorado, in 1984. Since the earliest years, he has been guided by his deep and broad understanding of log homes' basic building material. "We know what we're doing with wood," says Clyde. "I like taking timbers and turning them into a house that people can be proud of."

Whatever the log styles or log types, American Log Homes painstakingly dries its logs to 15 percent or less moisture content. "You don't have to worry about or allow for the shrinking, settling, or twisting you sometimes get with improperly dried logs," says Clyde. "Our logs are guaranteed." That quality commitment extends to how American Log Homes treats its customers. "We explain everything in minute detail," says Clyde. "We stay with them throughout the process." Adds Jeff Cremer, Clyde's son and company vice president, "We even get questions from people we sold to back in 1982 about how to care for their homes, and we'll help them out and do whatever it takes, also providing the best log-home maintenance products for the job."

The end result is incomparable homebuyer satisfaction. "There are a lot of happy people out there because they bought a log home through us," says Clyde Cremer. "We never forget that people are not numbers. They're individuals trying to build their dream homes."

American Log Homes
869 E. Industrial Blvd.
Pueblo West, Colorado 81008
800-518-6256
719-547-2135
www.TheCompleteGuideToLogHomes.com

Bibliography

Amburgey, A., Price, T., Williams, L. *Log Home construction and Maintenance Tips: How to Prevent Decay and Insects.* Atlanta: Georgia Forestry Commission

American Forest & Paper Association. 2005. National Design Specification (NDS) for Wood Construction. ANSI/AF&PA NDS-2005. Washington D.C.: AF&PA.

Anderson, L.O., and Sherwood, G.E. 1974. *Condensation Problems in Your House: Prevention and Solution*, U. S. Department of Agriculture. Forest Service. Agriculture Information Bulletin No. 373

Cassens, Daniel L & Feist, Undated. *WMC Exterior Wood in the South.* Madison: U.S. Forest Products Lab.

DeGroot, R.C. & Popham T.W. 1975. *Wood Moisture and Decay Problems in Recently Constructed Single Family Houses.* New Orleans: Southern Forest Experimental. Station

Forest Products Lab. 1966. *Weathering of Wood.* Madison: U.S. Forest Products Lab

Forest Products Lab. 1966. *Finishing Exterior Plywood.* Madison: U.S. Forest Products Lab

Forest Products Lab. 1970. *Wood Finishing: Blistering, Peeling and Cracking of House Paints from Moisture.* Madison: U.S. Forest Products Lab

Forest Products Lab. 1972. *Painting Outside Wood Surfaces.* Madison: U.S. Forest Service

Forest Products Lab. 1974. *Making Log Cabins Endure: Suggestions on Construction, Log Selection, Preservation and Finishing.* Madison: U.S. Forest Service

Harper, Robert Francis. 1904. *The Code of Hammurabi King of Babylon.* Chicago: University of Chicago Press. Reprinted by Lawbook Exchange Ltd 2000

Hepting, G.H. 1971. *Diseases of Forest and Shade Trees of the United States.* Madison: U.S. Forest Service

International Code Council. 2007. Standard on the Design and Construction of Log Structures: ICC 400-2007. Washington, D.C.: ICC.

Klenck, Thomas. 1988. *Cut and Dried* Popular Mechanics.

Koch, Peter 1972. Utilization of the Southern Pines. U.S.D.A. Southern Forest Experimentation Station Handbook Volume 1. Pineville: U.S. Department of Agriculture

Langsner, Drew. Swiss Chalets. *Fine Homebuilding Magazine.* October-November 1991: Pg 72-75.

Little, E. L., and Viereck, L.A. 1972. *Alaska Trees and Shrubs.* Washington, D.C.: U.S.D.A.

Mitchell, Nolan D. 1947. Fire tests of treated and untreated wood walls. Proceedings of the Annual Meeting of the American Wood-Preservers' Association, Portland, Oregon, April 22-24, 1947, Vol. 43. Washington D.C.: AWPA. pp.353-360.

Sherman, Joe. 1992. *Upscale or Down, Nothing Says Home Like a Log Cabin* Washington D.C. Smithsonian Associates

Sherwood, Gerald. 1984. *Wood Siding Types and Application.* Madison: U.S. Forest Service

Spier, John Cutting and Setting Common Rafters. *Fine Homebuilding Magazine.* October/November 2001: Pg 56-61.

Tobey, Jon 2001. The Care and Feeding of Wooden Decks. *Fine Homebuilding Magazine* April/May: 60-67.

Truax, T.R. 1959. Fire research and results at the Forest Products Laboratory. Report No. 1999. Madison WI: United States Department of Agriculture, Forest Service, Forest Products Laboratory.

Jones, Rudard A. 1975. *Moisture Condensation* University of Illinois at Urbana Building Research Council. Champaign: Building Research Council

University of Alaska 1971. *Building a Log Home in Alaska* Fairbanks: University of Alaska Cooperative Extension Service

U.S.D.A. 1955. *Wood Handbook.* Madison: U.S. Forest Service

U.S.D.A 1973. *Protecting Log Cabins, Rustic Work and Unseasoned Wood from Injurious Insects in the Eastern United States.* Washington, D.C.: U.S. Department of Agriculture

U.S.D.A Forest Service. 1975. *Properties of Major Southern Pines:* Washington, D.C.: U.S. Department of Agriculture

U.S.D.A. 1999. *Wood Handbook Wood as an Engineering Material General Technical . Report.* Madison: U.S. Forest Products Lab.

Index

Made in the USA
Lexington, KY
18 January 2010